The PSYCHOLOGY *of* DENIAL

The Complexities Of A Simple Idea

By

JACK WRIGHT PhD

ACKNOWLEDGEMENTS

My wife Alex was patient about how much time I spent reading and writing the last fifteen years of our 37 year marriage. She also gave me suggestions, including that for the subtitle: *Complexities of a Simple Idea*. My brother-in-law Don read through and discussed the whole book with me three times, and proved to be the best proof-reader for small errors and some clarifications. Heather McElwain, owner of Turtle Bay Creative, was encouraging while she shared her red ink and comments. She wasn't given the final run-through, so any further errors are my own. Then there are many friends on whom I tested ideas and sometimes chapters for their feedback.

The
PSYCHOLOGY
of
DENIAL:

The Complexities of a Simple Idea

Table Of Contents

*"True civilization lies
in the dominance of self
and not the dominance of other men."*

Chief Luther Standing Bear

PREFACE

The first time I noticed the importance of understanding denial better was when fighting to lose weight. I first thought that my mind was playing tricks. I felt like I was fighting with another person. I had finally noticed that I was obese (five feet ten inches and 310 pounds). I could look at my fat in a mirror and remind myself that, of the many factors involved in obesity, calories in and calories out were the areas in which I had the most control. Then I'd have a big meal with a sweet dessert.

I'm now 190 pounds and still losing, but I also still struggle to eat healthily. With concern for my health, and my bathroom scale encouraging me, I lost 40 pounds in the first six month of this journey. In the process, I began to understand my enemy: it was me. I found that most of denial results from unconscious mental programs learned over a great period of time. One of my programs illustrates how irrational such neural circuitry-driven programs can be, as this "other self" thought I needed to eat a lot.

Losing the 40 pounds appeared to have the most to do with eating a lot less. I was able to do that just by noticing that being full had little to do with how much I ate. My program to eat a lot, and be fat, had many facets, but central to its success was denying that I was overfull. I now feel overfull if I eat just a third of what I used to eat. I haven't had to give up any types of foods, and it's far easier for me to quit eating when I notice I'm full. I had been in denial about my own limits. I need to point out that I have lost my noticing of being overfull several times, but knowing I had been successful before made it easy to gain it back.

Once I recognized this denial in myself, I started to notice it in my clients. I found that my central task as a psychotherapist was to gently urge people to notice what they weren't openly recognizing, often some behavior that was eluding their awareness. This spanned from issues like how to relate to a spouse, to why too much alcohol isn't healthy, to almost every problem they presented. With this realization, I not only became more effective as a therapist, but also was better able to promote understanding.

I have been working on tracking this denial almost twenty years now, and *The Psychology of Denial* has been a work in progress for over ten. I'm now much better at identifying the underlying hurdles like the role of self-esteem, empathy, fear, and the ability to think critically. Many of the skills that aid us in our struggle with denial could have been learned in early childhood, but too many of us missed those lessons.

Now, late in my life, I've finally found happiness in being able, with time, to recognize and even change negative aspects of my personality. Achieving personal change isn't like receiving a burger from a fast-food restaurant; it takes patience. And with patience come success, self-esteem, and happiness.

The Psychology of Denial is based on interpreting my clinical and personal experiences through the lens of psychological science. That's not to say that it's experimentally researched. Denial is such an abstract concept involving so many aspects of human behavior that it won't lend itself to even a broad generalization from research. As Jerome Kagan at Harvard states, " . . . psychologists are not yet close to an accord on the basic elements of processes that underlie actions, beliefs, or emotions" (*Perspectives on Psychological Science,* March 2011).

Our ignorance has led to bad advice for parents. Punishment and other authoritarian styles of parenting have been supported for decades. Research has recently supported keeping children safe while letting them learn how to behave on their own. The authoritarian style, much like a permissive style and outright neglect, just teaches children to behave the parents' rules, or not to have rules, rather than to learn to establish such rules for themselves through critical thinking.

Few of us had parents, schoolteachers, bosses, or even spouses who taught us more through support than through criticism. Many of us have suffered from being graded and have been left wanting. We may have been expected to fix everything ourselves without authorities teaching us how to learn for ourselves.

Children attend schools where they are too often taught in an authoritarian way, which makes any misunderstanding their fault. Such perceived failures are discouraging for children. Feeling ignorant in such situations promotes denial, and when children or adults feel themselves found wrong or not good enough they protect themselves from the stress through denial.

In such an individualistic and authoritarian culture, self-blame can become a large part of the problem for many. Self-blame can even diminish punishment sometimes. The trouble is that self-blame limits our expectations and our risk taking. Then we easily feel stuck, and the stress of feeling stuck leads to denial. We all succumb to denial, which greatly inhibits our lives; however, we talk about denial in hindsight, yet we rarely recognize it at the time we are embroiled in it.

Many of our failures are determined by not knowing our obstacles to success. Like any task, accomplishment usually requires more knowledge than luck. First, we need to know about denial itself. Denial is natural and necessary for human life, and most of it is unconscious. We would be incapacitated by anxiety if we didn't deny things like unlikely elements of danger. However, many of us rarely think about issues like needing healthy food and adequate sleep. Sometimes we deny broad aspects of our lives like denying that we aren't happy, which limits our ability to change our situation. It's all too common that we deny we even have problems. Then, of course, they can't be fixed.

We call the physically limited "disabled." Such naming of persons with many abilities reflects our denial of ourselves being disabled in some ways. Our authoritarian world doesn't separate our person from our behavior, and we naturally fall into doing the same. In the judgmental and ostracizing world of authoritarianism, it easily feels wrong to let ourselves off the hook when our behavior is troubled.

It's difficult to separate our self (person) from our behavior when the rest of the world doesn't appear to believe that it's the right thing to do. Denial is a good deal easier than standing against the crowd. This is discussed more fully in Chapter Nine, but with patience and perseverance it works; it provides progress and its substantial happiness.

My hope in publishing this book is that many will overcome the despair of what is perceived as personal failures. When people learn that they can find the power to change their lives by taking the time to think through the issues presented in this book, the work becomes easier. I apologize for not being able to make the subject of denial easier. Sometimes it has felt like every sentence needed more explanation. Denial is a simple concept with many complexities.

My book will present applications of the psychology of denial to situations many readers may find of interest. I've worked four decades with clients who have struggled with denial, and I struggled along with them. Discussion between caring people will greatly enhance our understanding of the role denial plays in limiting our lives. As a character in one of Barry Lopez's stories (Apocalypse, in *Resistance*) puts the issue, we must breach "the indifference by which people survive." Clearly such indifference is denial, and a survival close to despair.

I'm quite open to hearing comments from readers that will improve my thinking about this important subject. It would be great to find an easier way to understand the psychology of denial. Readers may find some passages difficult and may need to do some serious thinking if my words are to be helpful. I believe the result will be worthwhile, leading readers to healthier cycles of life. I hope this book will set many on such a journey. Making progress is doing our best as human beings.

Jack Wright

*The man with insight enough
to admit his limitations
comes nearest to perfection.*

Johann von Goethe

INTRODUCTION:
FINDING HAPPINESS

It doesn't seem fair that some people are given lasting happiness in their first years of life. When they were children they had parents with adequate knowledge, personal security, economic stability, and a safe place to raise their family. Such parents were usually present, met their children's needs, and knew what to expect of their children as they reached each stage of their development. These circumstances generally produce happy children. Happy children develop their own personal security, excellent social skills, and do well in school regardless of their level of inherited intelligence. Such children are often able to maintain a long-term relationship, stay employed in an enjoyable field, and raise happy children.

Some of us may have met one or two such happy people in our lifetimes. They've usually suffered some difficult times, but they seem to roll with the punches well. The rest of us have to work at finding happiness. We worked basically without much help until psychological science became interested in happiness during the last two decades. We now have some help learning concepts like evidence that friends, not money, are most important to happiness.

Such information isn't enough. We also have to consider issues like whether our friends make us happy, whether we have much responsibility for our known failures, and whether we can change our lives. Having some knowledge of the limitations given to us by our parents can help us be patient with ourselves, but accepting that we always have a significant role in things that go wrong is crucial. Of course, we need to develop some personal security to be able to acknowledge such a responsibility.

How do we develop personal security if things are going wrong a good deal of the time? That takes thought, understanding and patience. We need to know that denial is a key element that limits our progress as humans. We may think we know what denial is, but a closer look finds denial to be ever present, and often severely limiting our chance for happiness. Denial inhibits our progress by shielding us from the truth. Yes, the truth sets us free, not to be perfect, but to change. Appreciating our ability to change is the basic step toward personal happiness. When we find we can change a behavior that has been found to hurt us, we find relief from despair.

If we've found happiness by our later years, even our mistakes, traumas, and tragedies can seem acceptable. It's as though we sense that we couldn't be who we are if we hadn't had those developments. The problem is that too few people seem to reach such a happy place.

The Psychology of Denial has been written to help with this problem, no matter what age we start to learn about it. Denial seems like a simple concept, and it is usually easy to see after the fact. However, it involves several central aspects of our personalities, which can make it difficult to overcome.

Much of our life consists of compulsive behavior. We don't mind when we're compulsive about breathing, keeping our balance, and many healthy behaviors. But we don't give enough credit to the difficulties around our compulsive negative behaviors. When we have engaged in a behavior for years, we would be in denial to think it won't take determined effort, knowledge, and patience to be successful in limiting, let alone stopping, such a behavior.

It's almost as difficult to change an unhealthy habit as it would be to change a healthy one. Try to learn not to blink when a bright light hits your eye, or not to form words in your mind. By the time we discover we have a difficult habit to change, we've probably practiced it for years and it's under the control of our neural structures. We are then easily discouraged from even thinking about changing what could be an annoying, or even life-threatening, behavior. We also add to the problem by developing what psychologists describe as "protective cognitions."

For example, we think—even argue—that not everyone dies from smoking or other such thoughts that protect a habituation. Such thinking is an aggressive form of denial. It's also denial to think we're really trying to quit a habit when we use a technique that has never worked. If we weren't working in the darkness of denial, surely we'd know that trying not to have another drink is like trying not to think about a purple cow. That's exactly the time that we would think about drinking.

Trying, like denial, appears simple, but it isn't. Trying feels like the natural thing to do when something doesn't go right, but it needs to be developed. We wouldn't be likely to succeed if we started a business without any study of what is known about business, including the one we want to start. Such an adventure could succeed, but normally we'd discover that we were in denial about the many pitfalls. Setting about to end a deeply engrained habit without some thought about what works is a similar denial. Most of us with a bad habit just *try* to stop it. When "trying" is thinking about stopping a negative behavior, we can experience something called a "rebound effect:" namely, that the habit gets worse. Simply trying and not *doing* is usually avoidance hidden in denial.

There are effective things to do about behaviors we want to change, but just trying isn't one of them. In fact, trying, when we think about it, is the opposite of quitting if we're not careful. Noticing our denial about effective approaches is how we can be successful. Asking about whether we consistently think about why we want a change may help us start noticing denial. Patience will be needed, as it's extremely rare for a person to stop enough of their use of denial to notice progress quickly.

Those of us who still smoke cigarettes today are a good example of this *trying* issue, in both senses of the word. Those without protective cognitions, like *my father smoked all his life and didn't die from lung cancer,* have usually tried several known-to-be-ineffective techniques. Gum, patches, not carrying their own cigarettes, and many more are rarely found to be effective. Meanwhile the Quit Line has receptionists with empirically supported programmed responses that have proven to be 80% effective. Basically they help us catch onto our denial.

Overcoming denial is difficult work that requires consistent determination, but it should be gentle work. Blame and exasperation are disguises of denial. Both come with labeling. It's well known that if we call ourselves not good, we'll have poor results trying to do better. If we're going to be gentle, we need to know what we're up against when we attempt to change. It's clear that bad habits are often driven by our accidently developed unconscious minds.

Progress aids our determination, and helps us understand that humans are never perfect. In fact, progress is human perfection. "I err, therefore I am human," most often credited to St. Augustine, and discussed by many, is apparently easily denied. Without a positive childhood background, repeated failure supports denial before exploration. Developing ourselves isn't easy because dominant aspects of our personality and character were set in place for us in our first years of life.

We neither chose nor trained our parents. We can have some control over the expression of our genes and biology, but they are a given in our lives, and are affected by many events out of our control, including obesity and other health issues. Current thinking is that we have only one-third of the responsibility for our lives; the rest is determined by genes and biology. This book is about what to do with the third we can control.

We are the most vulnerable when we deny our developmental history, but our limitations can usually be overcome when we accept our difficulties. Denying, for example, that we're pessimistic about our ability to adjust to the fast pace of the modern world easily leads to giving up. Giving up leads to feelings of life being out of control, and to despair. Being sure that we can't do something is most often protected by denial.

Such pessimism is particularly difficult because we're of course pessimistic about being able to change when we've had failure after failure. But even this attitude can be changed when we know how. Being able to influence and react to our environmental, genetic, and biological inheritance is like being able to drive a vehicle even if we didn't build it. It's called "agency," the power to exert reasonable control over our lives.

Feeling that we don't have control over our lives is a central cause of despair and suicide. Control is one of the four fundamental needs we humans have: The need for belonging, self-esteem, control, and meaningful existence. These are all easily disrupted at any age if we haven't developed adequate resilience with which to face ostracism from ourselves and others. Long-term exposure to ostracism, the exclusion and rejection that comes in many forms, depletes our ability to cope. Then we experience the opposite of our human needs: Alienation, unworthiness, helplessness, and meaninglessness.

Unlike a physical injury, damage to our essential needs often doesn't have a distinct pain and a clear remedy. When we add denial, which is easily supported by intense bad feelings, we sometimes make adjustments that cause even more damage. The pressure of our basic needs can lead to giving ourselves away in order to feel like we won't be further rejected. Alternatively, being true to ourselves is crucial to our sense of worthiness. Understanding denial, to be on guard in order to overcome it, becomes a critical issue if we're to maintain some control over our lives, and is crucial for finding happiness.

We may think we understand what the word *denial* means, but we may be missing the knowledge of how to stop living in denial. We're used to quick fixes, five steps to success, but denial easily defeats such attempts at happiness. Recognizing the role of denial in our lack of happiness is neither quick nor easy. The first step is to accept our attitude about mentally hard work. We may have been allowed to quit too easily in school, or found ways out of work with our distracted or unprepared parents. Fortunately, working on our own happiness becomes much easier once we experience some success, once we can see progress in our lives.

It's important to remember that our neurology is usually involved when we deny issues like driving too fast, eating or drinking too much, and other issues related to our ability to keep aware of long-term consequences. Denying that we can change our personality leads to thoughts that can also determine our outcomes. If we say to ourselves statements like *I can't do anything right,* then we easily feel stuck. Feeling stuck is often the result of denial and requires further thought. We may not have learned to think things through, especially with critical thinking. Life has become too fast-paced to just go with the flow; we need thinking to challenge our assumptions whenever our happiness feels diminished.

Many of us are addicts in a way: addicted to our comfort in a particular status quo. Change requires dealing with the anxiety that's a natural response to an unknown, like a new life-style. It's easier to deny that the problem is really important. Those of us who don't drink to provide our only happiness may have a difficult time understanding those with alcoholism. We then need to see that someone observing us may be unable to understand why we continue in a job or relationship that makes us look unhappy. It's simplistic but meaningful to say that we could be happy in our unhappy state because we fear change, and the possibility that we can't change.

Fear supports denial. If we haven't had failures and catastrophes of our own, we'd have to live in a cave not to know that they happen to others. Even in a cave, it would be important not to deny that a bear might want our home. Addictions don't change the reality of our fears; they just hide them from us. Doing nothing about our fears enables our problems. Successfully doing something empowers us.

Happiness is supported when we have a sense that we are not being stuck, out of control, or powerless. However, there are many things to fear over which we have no control; it's called human life. Knowing we're more of an agent than a victim is crucial if we're to be happy, or to reclaim our happiness. Even when we've been victimized, we can accept situations out of our control, and act on things we can affect. Human life is always open to growth, and progress can provide happiness no matter what our situation.

We can be poorly educated, have no work skills, still be stuck in poverty, and yet change our life for the better. We may still feel frustrated when we realize our car is a junker, and not a luxury vehicle. Comparison isn't to be denied, but it does need to be seen as a factor that can limit our progress. None of us can completely change our lives, but we can find happiness in feeling agency, having some control. Millionaires have been known to feel just as stuck as those feeling trapped in poverty when comparing themselves to billionaires who just built their tenth mansion next door.

When we find that the complexities of our life are leading us to denial instead of agency, we need to make some rules for ourselves. Sometimes we even need rules for our rules, like a rule that reminds us of a rule, or a rule not to be impatient when we forget a rule. For example, a person who has a poorly developed sense of consequences may need a rule to take time to think whenever doing something new. He may also need rules to be patient when he finds his well-practiced behaviors difficult to change.

When we find we have difficulty being patient with ourselves, it may also be clear to us that we have limited empathy skills. Many easily develop empathy in early childhood; however, for those who don't, it can be developed as an adult. Empathy has been described as trying to walk in another's shoes. To do that requires that we first know what it's like to walk in our own. When we haven't denied that serious change is difficult and a life-long process, we can develop empathy both for ourselves and others.

Some of us will have to learn perseverance to strengthen our patience and progress in our lives. Because change in our world often appears to come fast and easily, we can be misled into denying our own progress and a need for perseverance. Perseverance has to be practiced if it's to be valued. We can be fooled about gaining skills, friends, and material things too easily. Easy skills are rarely flexible or well developed, and easily gained friends and material things are rarely found to be satisfying.

Having a perspective on denial in our lives may feel overwhelming at first, but when we find the power to change our lives, we may find motivation to maintain this perspective. We don't like thinking of successful living as hard work, but it is for most of us. We must remember that meaning and happiness makes hard work feel easy. There is no greater meaning than to give the world better humans, and we can't deny happiness when we are those humans.

It wouldn't be wise to work at living all of the time. That would be too intense and would easily overcome the potential for joy in living. The problem with denial is that sometimes the obvious is the easiest to avoid. We may have become too accustomed to seeing our denial without really paying attention to it. The time to work at life is when we recognize mistakes. Noticing denial is a first step in learning from mistakes. Learning from mistakes is the human approach to happiness.

*Things turn out best for the people
who make the best
of the way things turn out.*

John Wooden

CHAPTER ONE:
CONSIDERING DENIAL

Geneticists have demonstrated that humans are not all that different from other animals. Fortunately for us, the small genetic difference is huge. General Semanticists have named this difference as our "time-binding" ability. All animals are able to learn from both success and failure, but humans are far better at learning from history, the successes and failures of those who have gone before. This ability is at the core of the science determining the distinction between humans and animals. Animals do pass on knowledge through their genes, but the human animal goes further than that, at least when denial isn't a problem.

This difference is especially clear when humans figure out that the lessons they learned from their parents or society are wrong. Humans are able to change social behaviors far more rapidly than other animals. As societies develop, not all change is found to be good, but the ability that humans have for change is a gigantic development in the evolutionary history of our planet. The processes of denial erode this incredible ability.

Sociologists and developmental psychologists tend to believe that most of us don't significantly change after our late adolescent years. This lack of human development is likely to be primarily caused by denial. Current research names part of the problem as a lack of "self-appraisal." Denial can constrain our lives, keep us from our great potential as human beings, and imprison us in despair. Many people are too busy just surviving to consider what they may be denying.

This doesn't apply to just the working poor who often hold two jobs to make enough for basic needs; those who are better-off are often caught up in issues that must feel like survival to them as well. Work and social involvements often leave people with little personal time. Many appear too driven to spend time on self-improvement, especially if it will take years. Consequentially, they often find that even having financial resources isn't enough to reduce the fear and insecurity that drive denial when they realize that change is needed.

An all too common example is the parent who is aware they have a relationship problem with a child, or children. They don't tend to deny the problem, but often become indifferent to the issue when some easy steps haven't worked. Relationship takes time, and time often demands large changes in a person's life style.

Emotions are a crucial aspect of human learning, and denial can be like an emotional blindfold keeping us from seeing ourselves in the mirror of life. Denial lurks in every aspect of one's life, but that needs to be seen more as a challenge than as a threat. With cursory views of successful lives, such accomplishment can appear to be luck, but it's likely that almost all successful people have done well with recovering from failure. Recovery from bumps in the road invariably includes overcoming denial, denial that we have the resources to either do better next time or chose a different path. We do need protection on the journey called life, but questioning how much is enough is very important.

We've used denial all of our lives and can slip into it easily. The issue is further complicated by the fact that denial can be a good thing. At several stages, children need to deny how impossible the world appears to them. Trust in their caregivers helps, and they need to be brave, but the dangers of life are too much for children. In a similar way, soldiers often need to find a way to deny how dangerous war is, or anxiety would incapacitate them. Denial is usually a temporary matter, like parents who, in order to function, need to deny that their children could die for a multitude of reasons. Caution is needed as denial can accumulate into a negative strategy for many of life's issues.

Denial is something for which we alone are responsible. When we avoid thoughts we think are intolerable, we bar ourselves from an improved life. Change can happen by luck, but any honest gambler will tell us that luck always runs out. There is no legitimate description for the life we could have had. But the changed life, fortunately, is up to us. It is the result of facing something that needed to be explored and possibly changed. Releasing thoughts that have been denied will help us find freedom and explore what else our life holds.

Noticing our denial requires a clear understanding that most denial is a deeply entrenched habit; it's unconscious. It's usually spotted by noticing a repeated negative behavior. We need to ask, "Why did I do that again?" Not being aware of the power of our unconscious mind over our behaviors is denial. If we're to discover freedom for change, negative denial must be stopped. We experience our mind as being tricky, and against our progress. Tricky it's not. We need to see the habit and how it's supported in our thinking, and in our not thinking.

It's all too common to feel stuck in an unhappy life. Those of us who claim to be depressed may just be bored or feeling stuck, a clear sign of denial. We often have trouble giving up on a plan that's no longer possible and deny that we can make adjustments. Moaning about what could have been is natural, but we can get caught up in it and become stuck. Friends can provide secondary rewards for a while, but they soon become tired of constant complaints. The opposite effect happens when someone recovers from personal disasters: lives become vibrant and interesting.

FACING ISSUES

The first step of most recoveries is to step out of denial. Whether we divorce, experience an unexpected death, sustain a major injury, or experience other setbacks, stepping out of denial means facing issues rather than lingering in the sympathy we get from ourselves and others. There is always more to a life than what we've planned. The harder life has been up to the beginning of a new situation, the more preparation we need in order to believe in ourselves enough to find and enjoy another path.

This is especially true when we've experienced failure. We need to check our personal history to see what it led us to expect of ourselves. When failure diminishes our expectations, we can usually find something missing in our parents' relationship to us, and that may have been reinforced by negative experiences in school. Children are especially vulnerable to normal life experiences like bullies, inadequately trained teachers, and the multiple negatives of experiencing poverty and other traumas. Ostracism, so common in an authoritarian environment, especially from a person of a dominant culture, is remarkably damaging to people of all ages.

In this fast-paced world, we must take time to reflect on our denial issues if we want to open up possibilities. One of the first issues for many of us is to confront our fast pace. Is it really necessary? Do we need all of the things that our busyness buys for us? It's now difficult for most of us to take time for self-improvement, especially if we're struggling to make ends meet, but we may find the result of making time to be dramatic.

When in denial it is difficult to take time for ourselves, in that we have become so accustomed to our routines. Both employment and raising children drive routines, and can clutter our lives with unthinking busyness. Recreation and other issues of self-care are easily lost in such an environment. Once we lift the curtain of denial, we will see possibilities for change. It sometimes takes a huge change for our lives to improve, but often fairly minor changes can help us gain healthier life-styles.

Often the goals driving our employment needs and parenting needs have been set in an isolated way, with little or no attention to our broader needs. Employment success and success at parenting are never enough when life is seen more holistically. Too often, especially in retirement, we find that our lives have become suddenly empty. Men are especially known to die within one year of retirement. Parents sometimes over-participate in their adult children's lives.

The denial problem here is that we often don't even know we despair. Despair is worse than depression in that it can be hidden in busyness. It can be denied by naming it tiredness, or even by just feeling numb. Both tiredness and numbness can be defended with self-blame. One of the problems is that when we feel like we never have enough time, we experience it as stress, not denial.

Humans adapt to stress very well when it doesn't incapacitate them, but that doesn't mean that it's healthy. When we don't seem to have enough time to make changes, we can find ourselves in a downward spiral regarding health and happiness. Denying such a despairing situation is a terrible mistake. Many of us will have to confront drug addictions and behaviors that have made our damaged lives acceptable. In a fast-paced life, the end is often known, but not in sight.

Our vision is diminished by despair in aid of denial. Soren Kierkegaard called despair "shut-up-ness," and claimed it took a "leap of faith" to escape the feeling. That was in the 1850s; it may be time for more of us to notice. We will need to be aware that a leap of faith isn't always successful. We might even undermine ourselves by choosing something without thinking the possibilities through. A well-considered leap of faith can be as simple as choosing to work less, be less busy, and focus on our mental and physical health more than our money.

Many issues overwhelm us today. For example, health issues can be very frustrating. The concepts of eating well and exercising are easy to understand. However, doing them can be complicated. We keep finding elements in our food that are slowly killing us. A red dye was found to cause cancer after being in our marketplace for a long while. A new chemical preservative, and there are so many of them today, can kill us down the road. There's nothing new about the problems. Long ago, we found that lead isn't a good sweetener for wines, much to the sorrow of Beethoven lovers. The wine he drank regularly was so sweetened.

Packaged foods are convenient, but we are finding that, like the problem with lead, food and petroleum products don't mix well over time. Currently, plastic baby bottles and cups are being recalled as being potentially cancerous. There may need to be major changes in our eating habits if we clear our minds of denial in the area of food.

Advertising has done well by food corporations, but it has also contributed to the denial of deadly down-the-road consequences, especially obesity. The science is clear: What you eat and how much you exercise determines obesity, but the issues are complex. There are genetic and parenting issues that make eating properly difficult. The food industry makes healthy eating even more difficult using sugar, salt, and fat to get us to eat too much. Exercise is complicated as well. Few would doubt that exercise is healthy, but it has to be weighed with other powerful factors.

Do you go for an hour's walk every morning or spend more time with your young children? In the here and now, is it better to go to the gym or spend the time at the office? All issues like these can be dealt with, but it is much easier, initially, to just deny them. Such issues are impossible to resolve if alternatives, especially apparently painful ones, aren't considered.

Such denied factors can be deadly. It's hard work to live well unless you're one of the fortunate few that were raised with a wellness model. Balancing work with health is particularly difficult in economically challenging times. And denial is often in support of itself. Denying that you have time for a healthy lifestyle often includes denying that you could change your budget. Many of us today seem to prefer having a nice house, even if we have no time to sit down to meals with our families, eat healthy foods that take more preparation, and take time for exercise.

FAILURES

Our parents may have told us that life is hard, but they were probably describing the struggle to survive or advance socially in a general way. When we consider denial, the issue is much larger. After survival, and more important than social success, personal growth determines happiness. Personal growth relies on careful self-appraisal, the opposite of a life lived in denial. We need to clearly evaluate our successes and our failures.

If our parents weren't successful developing in us a dynamic sense of our personal worth, personal growth is quite difficult at first. We might need some support for such a journey. Noticing needs for improvement is barred by past failure until we experience some success. Then mistakes can be taken as building blocks for future success, and an easier life.

With the complexity and difficulty of living, each of us will likely experience defeat. Denying defeat is a tragic waste of energy. Defeat denied doesn't go away, it accumulates. For those in denial, defeat typically implies stupidity or unluckiness. Both labels make further defeat predictable. In fact, expecting is a clever form of denial. It's best to think of defeat as experience not as failure. Of course, defeat doesn't feel like anything positive when it happens, which easily perpetuates denial.

If a person is to recover from self-deprecation following an experience of failure, the first step is to recover from denial, to evaluate our strengths and weaknesses. Once we recover from a defeat, we have a chance of thinking of ourselves as resilient. Labeling ourselves "resilient" will assist us in avoiding denial in the future. The possibility of failure won't be as likely considered an intolerable thought. Then we will have given ourselves some time to change course or at least make a softer landing.

If we've learned enough from several defeats, it's common to feel that we would choose to do most of them again for that knowledge. Being fired due to a lack of social skills, flunking out of high school due to a lack of seriousness, or developing a cigarette habit as an act of rebellion, are but a few of the many failures that actually can provide growth when we evaluate them.

Divorce is one of the biggest failures for which it's important not to miss out on the lessons to be learned. It's unusual for a second marriage to last if we deny the lessons. In divorce, it can be easier to blame the other party, but we won't learn much from that.

Relationship problems are always due to both parties. Not always to the same degree, but denying our part of the problem helps us avoid most of the gift such failures have to give. Large failures can be the wake-up calls we need if we're to step out of denial.

However, it isn't always big defeats that lead to denial. Life is filled with little things that don't go right, such a saying something that is found to be insensitive in a particular setting, or forgetting to keep an appointment. Each minor failure is an opportunity for a person's maturity. These "little defeats" are usually social issues, and are critical issues if we are to make progress with our social maturity.

We can recover from defeat over time by ignoring, but that is a limited recovery that often has more negative effects than positive ones. Suppressing thoughts of failure, we're less likely to recognize warnings of future situations. Without warning, mistakes are easier to make, and repeating mistakes easily causes despair. Sometimes we have to learn the same lesson over and over because we aren't aware of some factor of reinforcement, like enjoying sympathy for our dilemma.

SELF-ESTEEM

We need to be clear about our self-esteem issues if we are to escape the prison of denial, as they often determine how we act. Self-esteem begins developing within a few months of birth. An infant shows signs of thinking highly of herself within weeks of birth if she is well attended. Things all too regularly go wrong at this point, even without events that can be called abuse. Parents tend to be naïve about how much attention an infant requires. Attachment to others develops at this early point of life, and the long-term effects of the attention the infant receives are remarkable.

It seems safe to guess that a withdrawn infant who acts like he doesn't care if he gets any attention easily develops low self-esteem, or at least has less chance to develop high self-esteem. Similarly, a young child who is anxious and aggressive isn't likely to be developing good feelings about himself. Such personality issues usually affect people the rest of their lives.

If we predict from surveys of corporal punishment, only 16 percent of children develop from infancy without being regularly hit by caregivers. Psychologists generally don't approve of corporal punishment, as it has been found to diminish the quality of a relationship with the caregiver as well as to lower self-esteem. By the teenage years, a child who has been spanked regularly may be found on a continuum from rebellion against authority to unthinking acceptance of authority. We can anticipate low self-esteem on both sides of such a continuum.

False self-esteem can develop as a defense against pain behind both rebellion and unthinking acceptance. Any lack of honest communication from primary caregivers supports this form of denial. Further, denial easily feels like comfort for those with both feelings of low self-esteem and the anxiety that accompanies false self-esteem. Finding comfort in anything short of a solution to a problem exacerbates the problem. They come back if you drink them away. They just hide under prescription drugs. They go with you if you change environments. For those who have suffered from low self-esteem, it is important to accept life as difficult and focus on the positive effects of making progress.

Denial can easily lead to naïve optimism and false self-esteem. Both can limit our growth by hiding the need for change. Life experiences that affect our self-esteem determine whether we find personal issues exciting, defeating, or something in-between. When self-esteem is false or fragile in some way, we have usually been overprotected by parents, friends, our own denial, or a combination of such issues.

Denial can protect false self-esteem, and generate denial after denial, to protect the fabrication. We develop this fabrication by not receiving honest feedback in our younger years. If we artificially feel good about ourselves, it is easier not to recognize our obesity, negative personality factors, or anything that isn't immediately and frequently obvious failure. True self-esteem gives us the strength to see our shortcomings, and the will to do something about them. True self-esteem is built on our successes in life, especially those from paying attention to lessons learned.

The more we deal with our denial, the more true self-esteem, and the personal security it sustains, support our ability to change. Then we find that we can roll with the failures of life, and make the most from successes. False self-esteem uses denial to sap our resources for change. Recovering from defeat is especially critical because some of life's greatest lessons are learned in defeat.

When we deny our failures, we remain unaware of changes that we need to make to avoid repeating such mistakes. Self-esteem and personal security are most clearly involved in social errors, but are issues in many other circumstances as well. We must balance between these two aspects of personality, and between having too much and too little of either. Too much security is similar to too much self-esteem. Too much and too little are both false.

A criminal is the easiest example of someone with too much security and self-esteem. He usually thinks he's smarter than the police and not likely to get caught. Those who restrain themselves to their home warn us of what too little security and self-esteem can do to a person. Too little can also be seen in those who may be disappointed with life, but are afraid to try anything because they believe they will fail. The approach can feel easier than working at life. It is easier to be a pessimist because, as the joke states, things won't work out anyway. It's the consequences that aren't easier.

Security and self-esteem can become out of balance with each other as well. High self-esteem with low security is all too common in highly intelligent people who have problems with social adjustment. Low self-esteem with high security is common among those who were grossly overprotected as they grew up. Overprotection can feel safe, but it's demeaning at the same time. It has a dramatic further problem in that those who once protected us may die or move on. Finding substitutes for such protection normally just makes things worse.

Having at least one honest relationship is very important for those seeking to balance their aspects of security and self-esteem. Such a relationship can provide us feedback without making us feel attacked. Of course, critical observation needs to be invited or the feedback is less likely to be accepted. One can learn from uninvited observations of their behavior, but high security and self-esteem are often needed to appreciate the immaturity of the uninvited observer.

The right professional who provides trusted feedback can provide this relationship so critical to developing our personalities. Trusting feedback from any welcomed observer also fairly easily leads to less denial and more growth. Such feedback is often quickly found to be helpful and not attacking. Sometimes we luck out and have a soft beginning with a potential friend who understands the problem of our denial, and is patient with us.

Rarely, but possibly, we can develop wisdom and fight on our own, instead of engaging in flight. Denial is noticeable if we're willing to consider it. If we have a sense of being responsible for our lives, we can overcome denial and grow without the initial need for help. These moments, whether with assistance or on our own, are neither fun nor easy, as they usually come in the midst of an error important to a relationship. Perhaps we've said or done something that is hurtful or embarrassing to another.

Even mature people make such mistakes. Maturity is a continuum without limits on the positive end. Our self-esteem must be based on careful re-appraisals our whole life. When self-esteem isn't a dynamic factor in our lives, it can become a negative one. Psychology has researched this issue since the beginnings of scientific psychology, and currently there are roughly three new articles on self-esteem every day. The central issue is its role in determining our ability to act in our own best interest.

Some of the factors of effective self-esteem are emotional stability, belief in one's ability to act, and general good feelings about ourselves. Even if our parents did a good job raising us, we will need to frequently use self-evaluations to maintain personal success. That means we must not deny our needs for change, recognize failures, and continue genuinely believing in ourselves. The beginnings of change are usually the most difficult part.

Walking up hills is hard until you know you can do it. Practicing the clarinet is hard on everyone in the household until it becomes relatively enjoyable. Difficult tasks become easy not when they're finished, but when the effort is clearly rewarding. Symphony players work hard. They are known to practice at least four hours a day, and some days they probably don't want to. Money, prestige, and happiness usually prove to be an adequate reward making their decision easier.

The really hard part of life is facing and making decisions about the many difficult issues most of us face from time to time. We must exercise control to find personal happiness in contrast to what may be less important goal fulfilment. At such times, denial finds opportunity. Sometimes we need to recognize that set goals may not be in our best interests. They could have been set to please others, or for our own rewards that prove to be inadequate. Many of our difficulties in life are hand-me-downs.

Poor self-esteem, and the limited personal security that usually attends it, most often begins with our family of origin: namely, how our parents treated us. Did they treat us with respect? Did we feel safe around them and in our home? Was their opinion of us based on reality or wishful thinking? Did they teach us things like self-discipline or to obey irrational authority? Did they spend enough time with us to make us feel important?

These are just some of a long list of parent-relational issues that affect our personal security and self-esteem. Before we leave our parents, we experience other relationships, including siblings and anything from caring teachers to gang members. If we have experienced many negative relationships or hardships and are still making progress with our lives, we are to be congratulated. We've faced denial and are making the necessary adjustments to avoid pitfalls.

SELF TRUST

Trusting ourselves is critical to developing the self-esteem that aids us in our battles with denial. When we trust that we're honest with our life experiences, we've already learned that not denying provides us with wisdom for progress and resilience. Dwelling on negative memories isn't good, but denying that bad things have happened in our life is all too much like protecting ourselves by never leaving the house.

When we're in denial, we tend to work against trusting ourselves. Self-trust is based on regularly being successful in confronting the unknowns of life. We're trusting that we may not do something well, but that we will rebound from any mistakes we do make, and trusting that we're willing to pay attention to our responsibility for errors in living.

Sometimes this resilience is needed for mistakes that are out of our control. Successful business owners need to be out of denial when a Wal-Mart Super Store is built near them. For some, the only option is to do something other than their business, but seeing the problem helps with the adjustment. Others are able to adjust the emphasis of their business and do fairly well. Those blinded by denial suffer terrible personal and financial losses.

Death is an issue that is often out of our control. Being aware that it happens doesn't soften the blow, but prepares our adjustment, our resilience. A psychologist in the news suggested that the public's interest in dramatic deaths like plane crashes and earthquakes may relate to their denial of more realistic concerns like driving cars and obesity.

When we deny close-to-home issues, protections like driving defensively and eating wisely are much less available to us. If we deny that our marriage has problems, we often don't fix the problems in time. Denying that our children need more time, attention, and patience often leads to tragedies as well. Failure by denial is a major clue that we don't trust ourselves.

Even after feeling pretty good about ourselves, focusing on making progress is essential for happiness. When we view life as a work in progress, we will continue to see negatives as well as positives. We may still catch ourselves doing things like showing off in social situations, for example. We may know this to be a sign of insecurity, but we can also know we've improved in this struggle, and we're winning the battle. We're limiting denial.

Both old failures and new problems always have a chance to get us down, but if we don't succumb to denial, the strength of such failures and problems is diminished. We can feel good about still making progress with issues like false self-esteem and insecurity. They may never stop showing their ugliness in our lives, but they can be continually diminished as we develop genuine good feelings about ourselves. Out of denial we get better and better at seeing mistakes. Often we even see them coming in time to avoid them.

One significant clue that all isn't well with our self-view is defensiveness. Offending a genuinely secure person who has real self-esteem is difficult. Real and imagined social offenses are the usual ingredients for such attacks. Often, however, just subtle inferences can lead us to defensiveness. We usually don't take time to think through just what is going on when such negative events occur. It's safe to conclude that, when we feel defensive we're feeling threatened, but we usually deny the feeling. The denial then limits mature responses.

Reflecting on such experiences, we may realize that we felt caught when our defensive behaviors rushed up. It's not uncommon to find we've been bluffing that we're perfect in some way. With awareness, we can get to where we feel more empathy than threat for the immaturity of such attackers. All too often defensiveness looks like eight-year-olds arguing: "You're stupid." "No, you're stupid."

Denial can keep us from seeing the whole picture, which includes our immaturity, along with that of those troubling us. Fortunately, if we work on understanding our denial issues, noticing immaturity aids our development as a person. Then we've taken bars off our prison of denial. When someone implies that there is a better way to think about something, and we find ourselves rising to the defense of our approach to the subject, we can observe that we're feeling defensive. Sometimes we can even see that we are defending our insecure self, not our ideas.

Thinking that we're defending our ideas is just another trick of denial. If we allow ourselves to be tricked by denial too often, we end up not trusting ourselves. Defensiveness, taken as a clue to denial, can lead to understanding that it's an unnecessary part of making a good case for our ideas. We need to ask why we feel threatened by better ideas or even ones that are just different than ours.

Awareness of our defensiveness is especially helpful when there are political arguments. There is rarely any winning, and very little listening, in an argument regarding politics. If we're involved in such an event, it helps to stand back and watch. See if the issue isn't personal defensiveness, not the hope of persuasion. Not entering defensive relationships is a social skill that helps us trust ourselves at many other levels.

Even defensiveness that's hidden from consciousness can be detected, if we're on guard about it, as it usually has consequences. Sometimes we can diminish false self-esteem, which is often at the root of defensiveness, when we notice that we're jealous of someone's success. We can then question if we thought we could be best at everything. Then we can enjoy being who we are, rather than trying to be someone we're not. We will have matured, and positive change supports personal happiness.

MATURITY

We have to be patient with personal growth. Many elements of insecurity can be set up if any of our self-esteem isn't genuine. We may have to discover, and then inhibit, a desire to show people in social discussion how important we'd like them to think we are. This isn't an effective way to develop social relationships. Such discoveries can be painful and embarrassing.

Maturity doesn't by itself bring happiness. Growth does. Maturity is all too much like the concept of infinity: there's no end to it. That's good. When maturity is a journey instead of an accomplishment there can be less comparison and defensiveness. What we learn to trust in ourselves when we fight being in denial is that we are able to mature. Denial is like a self-imposed cage restricting our lives. Yes, others handed us some of the bars. Some even helped place them around us, but we may have denied that the bars could be removed. When we learn to trust facing our fears, we learn there is more to life. We do need to be patient with our deeply entrenched denial enemy. It does get easier when we can spot a need for our change in a social setting. For example, if we recognize that we're talking more than others, we can change such a behavior right away.

Learning to discover denial in our lives is learning to be true to ourselves. In *Hamlet,* Shakespeare presented that being true to yourself was "above all." Being true to ourselves is a critical element if a person is to mature, and maturity is the yeast of happiness. We don't mature very well, if at all, when denial has us caged.

By the time many of us find ourselves to be prisoners of denial, our cage has many bars, and each bar has a lock. Unlocking one bar doesn't necessary let us out. Unlocking one just helps us know that more can be unlocked. As the bars are diminished, more light enters our lives and we have more motivation to free ourselves and grow into the person we can be.

STEPS THAT MAY DEEPEN UNDERSTANDING

1. Notice if you've been feeling stuck in any areas of your life. If you have not been successful quitting smoking, overeating, fighting with friends and family, it may help to write the issues down and choose one on which to focus your attention. Follow this up with notes about when these failures arise and what your attitude is about them.

2. Notice if you've unsuccessfully tried to change any behavior and then just quit without looking for a new solution. Again, writing down a list will

help raise your awareness. Notice your attitude about not looking for solutions.

3. Clarify if your self-esteem needs to be developed before you will believe you can change. Perhaps write down how you describe your self-esteem now, and how you would like to describe it. See if you have any ideas about how to change your self-esteem.

4. Imagine the worthwhileness of personal change in order to think about the years it may take to accomplish. Ask yourself if you see an adequate importance of your need for change to be patient about it for years.

5. Read the following chapters to understand the several issues that affect personal change.

Ain't that just like living?
What ever happened to real life?

Mose Allison

CHAPTER TWO
CRITICAL THINKING

Critical thinking can be thought of as our human ability to seek and consider different approaches and further information than that which is common to us. Critical thinking is foundational for recognizing denial. It means considering that we're wrong about something we believe, or just haven't considered some more effective alternative. Sometimes critical thinking is called "divergent thinking" when we're looking for new solutions. When divergent possibilities are considered, we can often converge them into successful problem solving.

Critical thinking can be helpful during conversations with colleagues and friends. It supports the social skill of genuine dialogue. It's also required at times when we recognize that something may be wrong in our lives, especially when we feel stuck. Critical thinking opens possibilities and new insight. Not using critical thinking is one of the most obvious expressions of denial today. Personal change is usually in collusion with anxiety, and positive outcome expectation is crucial if we're to stay out of denial about our abilities to change ourselves.

It's important, though perhaps painful, to come to a realization that facing the mistakes we're making is better than entering despair. Despair is a quiet retreat from a full life. It's a short step above depression, and just short of a life of indifference that we sometimes use to survive the complexities we face. Our own mistakes are the ones over which we have the most control, because we can have hope and confidence in our ability to change. To be confident about personal change, we have to be successful in recognizing how denial has been blocking or human abilities.

Emotional pain may be why critical thinking is often missing in education. When teachers have believed in their approach to a subject for decades, it's very difficult for them to consider errors made over so much time. We are far more comfortable thinking we know something than when we're not sure or even suspicious of being in error.

Too often education today involves memorizing what is thought to be truths. It's even hard to remember such information because we've memorized what we we're learning more than we've processed it. With only vague memory of the facts presented, we usually end up with the dominant Euro-Christian slant about history and science if we don't use critical thinking.

Because educational institutions often don't demonstrate critical thinking to us, we may find it natural not to consider alternatives when we find our lives aren't going well. The value of true information is often found in retrospect. Holding on to misinformation enhances ignorance. Comfort with the status quo might also have been modeled in our homes. Then how unlikely is it that we will use critical thinking when we feel stuck in a job, a relationship, or other difficult places?

HINDRANCES TO LEARNING

Even when we consider other information or actions, complexity arises in our consciousness. The threat of failure may immobilize us. We will be entering uncharted territory. Insecure about new decisions, we're likely to find it difficult to think thoughts and behaviors through clearly. Our working memory gets tied up with concerns other than understanding the truth.

Personal change is a lot of work, but that isn't usually what drives our denial. A feeling of hopelessness easily strengthens denial in the face of complexity. A quick example would be to consider leaving a poor employment situation. It's unlikely that the solution would be simple.

We would likely have needs for financial security. We may also find we have self-esteem issues. Do we believe we can still sell ourselves? Do we need more training? Can we afford training? Do we have time to do it? Would we be successful in learning new skills? Complexity after complexity becomes tiring and anxiety provoking; denial is an easy relief, and then we're stuck.

When our history doesn't include critical thinking, we are forced to try something for which we have little cognitive support. It helps if we have a sense of what our despair feels like. When we notice anxiety about whether we are able to change for the better, we can use our despair to motivate further facing of these complexities. With just moderate maturity we know that despair doesn't help with a solution. It's at least a delay, if not outright giving up. In contrast, having good information about deficiencies in our development may help us be patient enough to find solutions. Known problems can be fixed, or at least worked around.

EDUCATION

Cookbooks may help in the kitchen, but they aren't appropriately used in education. Teachers need to be mentors showing us how to think, to make our own modifiable cookbooks. A course in English, for example, needs to be about teaching students how to express themselves clearly, not about memorizing boring rules for a test. Math needs to be less about memorizing rules, and more about thinking how to express numerical relationships. And history books are misleading if the issues of bias and perspective aren't also taught. Only a few of us received this kind of education at any level.

Each course needs to be an application of critical thinking. Some of us were fortunate in that we had teachers who didn't ask for agreement but rather for careful consideration of the evidence. Even preschool children need an educational environment in which they learn more about discovering what works than what brings punishment. Finding out what works by experimentation is far better than finding out what you can get away with.

A good education in how to learn, and what learning is for, can make life an exciting instead of discouraging challenge. Whatever our level of intelligence, we can feel we make progress with that which confuses us. We can modify our beliefs when they're not working well for us. We can think for ourselves.

The education experience for many today too often ends at high school or earlier, or even after graduate school. Perhaps we lose interest in a subject instead of finding interest in exploring it further. Perhaps we haven't learned to think about it when it isn't being taught to us. When we've learned to think critically we are more likely to see education as a lifelong process.

EARLY CHILDHOOD DEVELOPMENT

By the time children are one year old, their attachment style is in place. Children may be generally withdrawn from attachments, not expecting much from anything; anxious about attachments, nervous about whether they will work out; or secure in their attachments, able to adjust without denial. Using critical thinking as adults, we can assess information to know how difficult change will be, depending on the attachment style we developed as children.

The first step for consciously making positive changes in our lives is self-appraisal. Most of us aren't very realistic about this approach to ourselves, or at least not consistently. The quality of our self-appraisal determines our growth. As philosophers have long known, critical thinking is a crucial element if we're to find any knowledge even close to the truth. We have to determine our motives, biases, assumptions, and prejudices, if our self-appraisal is to be helpful.

It's not difficult to determine whether our attachment style is withdrawn, anxious, or secure. More difficult is determining whether we're biased, making assumptions, or harboring prejudices. Most of these problems are developed in early childhood and are well entrenched in our unconscious before we're even teenagers. Self-appraisal usually needs to include asking for constructive feedback. People from a dominant culture may be especially surprised at what they hear if they ask. Many of us may have to work on keeping our defensiveness in check in order to hear such information, even when it isn't stated with hostility.

Critical thinking involves open-mindedness, and seems to be considered an immoral state by some organized religions. Many organizations often appear to demand their members think similar rationalizations about beliefs, a fear-driven defensiveness. This could be a result of insecure attachment. Critical thinking rarely leads to many people thinking alike.

Rationality often has a similar reputation. Sometimes we need to consider emotion with rationality if there is to be learning. Caution needs to be considered to avoid giving emotion a dominating position over reason. Using critical thinking, we bring a balance that includes skepticism, and full concern for the weight of evidence of each situation.

We may have experienced issues in self-dialogue and dialogue with others due to a lack of critical thinking. Current arguments on news shows and even around some dinner tables demonstrate more emotion than wisdom. Often, our attitude speaks loudly of an unwillingness to know the truth. This lack of critical thinking supports denial that we may not always be right.

Accepting that we may be wrong, let alone actually changing our mind, does take some courage in this modern denial-filled world. Mind changing is too often criticized. Politicians get roundly criticized if they change their minds about an issue important to their constituency. Current research finds that most people look to confirm their currently held views, and have little concern that they may be ignoring new evidence. Francis Bacon was concerned about this issue in 1620. Twenty-two centuries ago, Socrates believed that knowing that we don't know is crucial to self-appraisal. He also believed more in dialogue than in argument, thus he embraced critical thinking and eschewed denial.

POSTMODERN INSECURITY

The postmodern label, describing a world where modern has gone too far, isn't a comfortable one for either liberals or conservatives, but it fits with the humility demanded by critical thinking. Modern world dwellers acted as though they owned the earth. Some now think it was leased to humans and that the lease can expire. Those in the sciences were often confident that their rules of rational proof were adequate. The products of mechanics were thought to be able to replace nature. In the post-modern world, we are opening our eyes slowly about the complexity and chaos that has been denied.

Ayn Rand's philosophy, Objectivism, though dedicated to rational thinking lacked objective thinking. One of her main followers, Leonard Peikoff, expressed that all we need to save the world is to think. The movement has few followers today as their thinking looked more like brilliant rational defensiveness than clear thinking. Membership in their group was terminated if any thinking diverged from Ayn's individualistic philosophy. It seems that the objectivists were only objective within their own paradigm. They didn't appear to understand issues like biases, prejudices, and the role of emotions.

Critical thinking can bring us to understanding the limits of individualism and our need for community. It might help us see that we don't own the earth; we belong to it. When thinking about how to care for the earth and its peoples, we cannot deny the population crisis, the water crisis, the nuclear crisis, and all those things of the postmodern world that go bump in the night. It's beginning to be seen that individual success isn't enough for survival. Governments seem to have made the majority of people feel powerless, but the absurdity of many uncaring behaviors may force more of us to think things through critically, get out of our fears, and out of denial. Then we may see a broad change in our history.

Most of our world is changing so fast, it leaves many of us experiencing it as threatening. It's impossible for any individual to keep up with so many changes. How do we eat right, exercise more, not use so much oil, and teach our children that their studies need to be balanced with their electronic indulgences? Threat often supports denial, not critical thinking, and denial doesn't find solutions.

People in the modern world now appear to have been naïve about their faith in science. Yes, science can do many things over time, but its goals aren't always clear and our common morality may not be strong enough to offer some of the controls it needs. Logical Positivism, like Objectivism, tried to state that only measurable facts were relevant. Some of its methods of proof are still used, but sciences are now wary of its limitations.

Karl Popper corrected Logical Positivism with his demand for falsifiability. He stated that science needed to limit itself to information that can be proven false, which led to him being called the father of modern scientific method. We can also call him an advocate for critical thinking, though it appears that he thought all truths could be proven. Many beliefs aren't measurable in any scientific way. Beliefs may hold truth, but people do need to hold them accountable by noticing their effects, and considering alternative views. Beliefs that aren't falsifiable still need the restraint that denial-awareness brings.

Even those not trained in the philosophy of science have a sense of dread when science appears to be getting ahead of human understanding. Some of us worried about physicists being "fairly sure" that the first test of an atomic bomb wouldn't set the atmosphere on fire. Arrogance and curiosity seemed to drive the experiment. More recently, physicists were "confident" that our world wouldn't collapse if they were able to produce a black hole in their huge accelerator.

The excitement of the positive possibilities in the sciences easily aids people's denial of the need to prove that huge experiments won't go badly. It may help that more people in this postmodern world are stepping out of denial regarding the fact that the nuclear age isn't all positive. There is a sense that unavoidable fears might awaken us. We might again have more appreciation for critical thinking in the sciences.

COMMITMENT WITHOUT DENIAL

We wouldn't be able to function without commitment to our beliefs. Critical thinking isn't meant to unsettle us, or restrict our lives. Knowing what we believe gives direction to our lives. It's our rationalizations that get us in trouble, blinding us with denial. Rationalizations are defenses of our beliefs that can become too rigid without critical thinking. Alfred North Whitehead puts the matter succinctly: "In philosophical discussion, the merest hint of dogmatic certainty as to finality of statement is an exhibition of folly" (Preface, p. x, *Process and Reality,* 1933).

Whitehead was a mathematician influenced by the failure of Newtonian physics at the hands of Einstein. He discussed philosophy, education, and other issues related to critical thinking. He argued in favor of believing unscientific things like the existence of God, but required that any belief have a committed concern for what is true.

Fear renders all too many of us into the folly of rigid thinking. Belief without denial is flexible. It allows us to keep up with the times, new information, new worries, without losing its power to guide our lives. When we're secure about the flexibility of our beliefs we don't tend to jump on each new bandwagon that comes along. We evaluate our thoughts and experiences. When we grasp and defend each new idea, this suggests that our beliefs are empty, or at least not guiding us adequately.

To use critical thinking as a guide in our lives requires more self-confidence than fear, more awareness than denial, more seeking, and less defensiveness. We may have grown up eating processed meats, but we can limit such a habit with knowledge of the effects of common contaminants found in them. It will be important to notice that if we fear such complexities, denial is more likely to cloud our responses.

If we use critical thinking, we are less likely to have problems with fear in the postmodern world. The history of the human race is replete with drastic demands on our beliefs in reality. We've killed both philosophers and scientists for bringing us some of these messages. It is human nature to have fear of the unknown. Sometimes it's overcome by careful trials over time; sometimes by avoidance.

The postmodern world is testing our ability to face challenges to our beliefs. Rapid scientific advancement, especially the Internet, is pushing our intellectual abilities. There has been little training to think clearly under pressure. The dominant race especially has acted as though few adjustments are needed, and that they have little responsibility for the troubles of the world. Science has come a long way in the last two centuries of this human race. Morality, overcoming the ignorance of bias and arrogance, hasn't done as well.

Now we find we don't even have words for some of the wonders we face. Astrophysicists are finding that basic assumptions like infinity are inadequate for their discoveries. Stephen Hawking warns us that we should be careful seeking other life forms as they might be far advanced from us, and would likely be colonizers like we have been. Our research in genetics draws us in with great possibilities for health, but the advances appear to far outstrip our moral ability to handle all of the consequences.

Critical thinking is not wandering in confusion; it's clear thinking that actually supports comfort in our beliefs. Yes, we need to consider that our beliefs are wrong, or at least may need strengthening from more knowledge, but they are still our guides for living the best we can. Our reality is evolving, making it important for us to find security in our wandering more than our finding. *The Psychology of Denial* argues that progress *is* perfection in human life. Few of us would argue that we're actually perfect, but sometimes we act and think as though we are.

PARENTING

The parenting we first receive is our earliest and often most long-lasting education. Research suggests that many parents don't understand the importance of their role. Even the genes we start with aren't a sure thing. They need the right environment if they're to be effectively expressed. The first two years of our lives is the easiest time to learn the rudiments of critical thinking. We can learn that smiles work better than screams if our parents are on the job.

By two years of age, we can learn that we don't have as much control over our world as we thought. As we develop more words, we can start using verbal logic that, with parental guidance, greatly advances our ability for critical thinking. Parents can ask us why something didn't work, and what other ways we can try to approach the issues. With time spent on such issues, and not too much chaos in a child's life, teenagers can develop with few troubles and feel effectively in charge of their lives, not dependent on the control of their parents.

As parents, we need to learn that we aren't effective if we just teach our children to obey us. Our children are out of our reach quite soon, and need to be able to think for themselves. We can more easily control our behavior if it's for our long-term pleasure, not that of others. When adults do things like choose to have sexual affairs, they often think they're just breaking some rules. It's likely they haven't had adequate parenting to develop the neurology need for quickly examining consequences. Critical thinking might warn them of the personal pain that usually results from affairs.

Critical thinking learned from childhood feels natural, helpful, and not limiting. Denial reigns when critical thinking hasn't been well developed. The neurology of helpful thinking is best put in place the first year of our lives, but that often doesn't happen. It isn't just parent neglect or drugs, but also parents are too busy to attend to children's needs. The norm for time with our children is down 60 percent from what it was in the 1960s: now just ten hours a week.

Information on parenting also varies. Paediatricians have differed on how to respond to an infant's cries. The point has been missed that the infant is learning consequences: I cry and I get food, and so on. Surveys have found that parents responded to cries of male infants some ten times more minutes later than those of female infants. That may account for why young males have more trouble with the law, more serious accidents, and don't generally do as well as girls in school. More extreme neglect than that may account for the fact that some criminal males have been found to have gross underdevelopment of the neurology of consequences.

Prevention of limited critical thinking starts by educating parents that their parenting greatly determines the success of their child. All the money that can be used for education, all the genetics for success, all the counselling for rehabilitation, these have less effect than consistent parenting from the start. Critical thinking develops social skills, which have been found more important for life success than intelligence.

Our children need to be encouraged to think about whether an approach is working, whether something else might work better, and whether a behavior will make them happy in the long run. The biblical dictum to love our neighbor like we love ourselves is often corrupted by not knowing how to love ourselves wisely. It's more difficult as adults, but crucial, to learn how to be happy in the now while not denying the need for delayed gratification if we're to be happy in the future.

SOCIETY

As we mature, our experiences within society will further shape our critical thinking or our lack of it. Society can be seriously troubling if we don't know how to evaluate its teachings. Education and parenting have left many without the skills they need to navigate society's twists and turns. Surveys find that adults in the United States don't know their own history, don't understand government or economics, and aren't careful with their choices about money, relationships, education, and much more.

If we were to follow general society's lead, we wouldn't read or talk about thought-provoking matters, or at least not with serious information. We would eat, sleep, and exercise poorly, and likely die before we're seventy without anything near the full use of our brains. Those of us gathered in such a society rarely seek news in depth, rarely read a thoughtful book, and prefer to see what others think is important. Biased presenters of information about politics, society, religion, and such, would often be able to claim us as followers.

In this society where ignorance competes with the mundane, those of us with critical thinking skills may feel isolated. Those of us caught up in the madness of a society without thinking are unlikely to associate with people who cause us the discomfort of wondering about other ways of seeing things.

Yes, critical thinking has to be maintained when those around us don't reinforce it and it causes distress. We become strangers in the midst of a norm. The distress is ours, as the others turn us off and avoid our seriousness. We often end up either bored or alone. We discover that we're abnormal. Being all right alone is necessary, but a few friends helps immensely.

We maintain critical thinking by awareness, by avoiding denial. Critical thinking solves some problems and raises some others, but it provides the only genuine satisfaction in life when we accept that progress is all we can know. When our progress results in developing personality and social skills, happiness clearly rewards the task.

When we're not anxious about what we don't know, we maintain our critical thinking by realizing that it is responsible for what we've learned. Out of school, we learn by finding elements of society that challenge us, fascinate us, and facilitate our development as mature human beings. In developmental psychology, we study maturation from our prenatal period to our death. We find that development is for good or ill. We're kidding ourselves if we think we don't change.

CHANGE

The Psychology of Denial is about how denial limits our ability to make conscious positive changes in our lives. We change all the time to one degree or another, with much of it unconscious and out of our control. We often see ourselves in some mirror of life and wonder how we got the way we look. It isn't just the shape of our body; some mirrors reflect the shape of our minds and relationships.

Change appears very difficult, but the core problem stems from time needed to make such changes. Society tends only to honor the quick changes people make. Deep and lasting change demands constant critical thinking. Reversing compulsive negative habits is the clearest illustration of this issue. Those in psychology have known for decades that successive steps toward a behavioral goal each need reinforcement. The goal reached will be its own reward.

Alan Marlatt at the University of Washington studied the issue of behavioral change for years with regard to alcoholism. He promoted the concept of "harm reduction." Drink less. Take pride in progress. Let progress build self-esteem. Self-esteem helps with the patience that is needed for further progress. Problems like drinking too much do need to be brought under control in time for a life well lived, but we'll never finish with problems in our lives. Steps of change are how we grow until we die.

Maintaining our status quo can be taken as reducing fear, but the opposite is true. Fear is only hidden by denial in such conditions. Fear can feel reduced with denial, including expressions of denial like drinking too much, but we need to be aware that it's really life that is then reduced. Critical thinking is the technique that prepares us for change in our lives. For example, using critical thinking, we can notice that our credit card balances should worry us. Then we can figure out that we don't need to fear a growing debt problem; we need to do something about it.

A big impediment at the do-something stage of change is thinking that there's nothing to do. Such thinking is always denial, and is facilitated by not having learned to do our critical thinking well enough. Usually we need to make major changes to improve a situation, like giving up our house instead of borrowing against it. Such thinking is frightening, but facing such fears keeps positive possibilities alive.

Thinking about such a situation is very complex. Our pride is often strongly involved. Our past situations may have made us feel optimistic about our future. Other people may have been implying that our thinking is all right because they are also involved in such situations. At such a point, our thinking needs to include knowledge that situations change beyond our control, that we change, and that change isn't necessarily for the better.

Change performed using critical thinking may not save us from some disaster, but it will certainly significantly add to what we learn from such a failure. In a world where we have little control beyond some control of our individual life, learning from our errors supports our ability to do better. Anything less will just feel like bad luck and be of no help at all in our pursuit of well-being.

THE LIGHT BRIGADE

Those of us using critical thinking wouldn't make good soldiers. The Prussian soldiers under Napoleon may have sensed they were in a precarious position, but they were to follow the leader, to do or die. Many United States citizens, including a majority in the recent Congress, appear to be like good soldiers. Following is certainly simpler than thinking for ourselves. At least we're less likely to be singled out for criticism, and we'll have company if things don't work out.

Not recognizing the power of one in this large but socially shrinking planet supports denying the power of individuals using critical thinking and dialogue for world change. The power of groups is in the accumulation of thought. Groups using critical thinking don't have to agree to come to a consensus. There can be, for example, many reasons not to bring a nation to a certain war. Hearing out the reasons could diminish the fear that sustains denial and confuses the decision.

Some of the leaders we tend to choose to follow when we don't use critical thinking are legal "persons": corporations. We let them tell us things like which drugs are safe. We let them spend millions of dollars influencing Congress to protect their turf. We let them poison our children, and seduce us into obesity for profit.

Our only control over such powerful entities is the power of one. One person with one vote works for controlling corporations as well as government. Not buying the corporation's product doesn't always work. We don't always get what we want voting in elections either. However, if enough of us have consensus, powerful entities bow to our will, but we have to have critical thinking about such issues.

Even when action fails, we will feel like we did the right thing. When we don't yell and scream, we encourage others to think differently by not stimulating their defensiveness. Consensus builds the power of one into the power of many. Groaning about feeling powerless does little more than support despair, and then denial appears to be the solution. Sometimes taking action requires courage, but often it just means acting on our own critical thinking about the situation.

If we are to follow the dictum that we should to our self be true, then we must face the unknown and the uncertainty in our lives. Accepting what others have told us without critical thinking isn't being true to ourselves even if we later come to believe what was told. Usually we will find that we will always have more to learn and that the learning affects us. The situation may initially feel like too much, and we'll have to trust our progress and be patient.

With critical thinking we will surely find improved contentment, if not consistent happiness. The process starts with enhancing the security we were given in childhood, or building it for ourselves. No matter what our level of general intelligence, or our physical features, we were supposed to feel bright, beautiful, and beloved by the age of five. Learning about the psychology of denial proffers help for those of us left with the task of making up for deficits in our personal environment. Then we can manage the anxiety of thinking critically until its rewards are clear.

STEPS THAT MAY DEEPEN UNDERSTANDING

1. Consider what your school experiences taught you about the importance of critical thinking. Was there much consideration for opposing ideas, or even discussion of the facts that led to conclusions?

2. Work on becoming secure enough to question many of the things you've been taught to believe. What you believe about yourself is especially important to consider. Reconsider your religious, political, and economic beliefs: how you came to believe them and how they affect your life.

3. Notice if the fear of making mistakes limits your possibilities. Are there things you haven't tried to do again after a failure? Do you still beat yourself up over past mistakes?

4. Treat yourself as more important than your beliefs. At least consider what you would do if you felt more capable. Then make yourself more capable.

5. Regulate your emotions and rationalizations while you question your beliefs. Quiet yourself with pleasant thoughts and deep breathing when a thought has upset you. Challenge your rationalizations when you feel very confident in them. Question whether it's best to be correct or to learn.

*Nothing is so firmly believed as
that which we least know.*

Montaigne

CHAPTER THREE
COMPULSIVITY

When we understand that our behaviors are neurologically driven, we can see that all behaviors are compulsive in a sense. We usually reserve the word *compulsive* as a descriptor of negative behaviors: behaviors that are difficult to change. However, we can understand denial better when we notice that our practiced behaviors can be called compulsive. We just don't usually want to stop them if they have positive results. Noticing that we have compulsive behaviors is important as they reflect limited awareness. They are quite subject to denial.

Putting the transmission into park before getting out of a vehicle is a positive compulsion that most drivers have. If we're compulsive about something like washing dishes, we may have a compulsive disorder, but one that doesn't need to be entirely stopped. However, inhibiting a damaging compulsive behavior is an issue in which developing awareness, acceptance, and patience, is important for limiting our denial.

Compulsive behaviors become a serious problem when they are used to mask deep feelings. Used as a technique of denial, the consequences of compulsive behaviors can be a huge limitation on our lives, even resulting in death. First of all, the feelings avoided usually are something we can effectively use to improve our lives if we address them. For example, alcoholics often fear they can't be happy except when they're at least moderately inebriated. That leaves them not learning much from pain. Like not paying attention to the lessons of history, pain unattended tends to repeat.

Like most who enjoy the effects of any intoxication, alcoholics are often confused about their situation. They may experience unhappiness and not really know why. Unhappiness is a common experience for all of us, with both fixes and adjustments that can be accomplished. Unhappiness requires some personal work. Sometimes we're given happiness, but most of us have to work at it. The work is usually about addressing denial issues. We may not have learned how to achieve happiness. That's especially a common experience when we start life happy and then experience change. It can be frightening when life isn't what we expected.

When in denial, not much is learned, and the primary feeling is often fear of failure. When we've been overprotected in some way, we don't know much about resilience and don't feel agency, the power to change our lives. We may need some support to overcome masking and denying deep feelings. We usually have to start with a small step, but finding any ability to change can be a powerful experience.

AVOIDING DENIAL

Compulsive behaviors often don't have large negative consequences, which means we easily tend to just put up with them. They are guarded by the frustration that comes when we try to stop such behaviors. We defend our denial about a behavior's negative consequences by calling it a *bad habit*. For many of us, somehow that implies that we're stuck with the behavior. It just becomes one of our negatives that we feel we can accept. The biggest problem with thinking this way is that our negatives tend to accumulate and can eventually tip the balance of our lives toward despair.

Whether or not our compulsive behaviors are disorders, the central issue is denial. Experts make treating compulsive disorders sound complicated. That may have to do with the general lack of success in treating such behaviors. Such counsellors may possibly need more understanding of denial. We are finding genetic roots to compulsive behaviors, but that doesn't mean they can't be changed. Their negative effects are clear, and they reinforce themselves. They are well-practiced behaviors that protect our denial of conscious and unconscious fears.

When we notice negative consequences that are some of our worst problems, it's valuable to notice our denial factors that relate to the issue, such as drinking too much, overeating, anything known to be a negative behavior. We rarely seriously answer ourselves when we ask *why do I keep doing this?* Not seeking a serious answer to our question protects our denial from the underlying deep feelings. The question may even aid denial by letting us feel like we're doing something about our problems.

AN ILLUSTRATION

One behavior that challenged me was picking at my cuticles. I didn't focus on the problem until I experienced success with an overeating issue. I think I began picking after I started seeing clients as a psychologist. My guess is that picking at my cuticles was a distraction from stress, but the behavior became so compulsive that I didn't need much stress to cause the behavior. I even began to treat boredom as a stressor. My fingers sometimes bled, but frequently were just red, and painful.

Just thinking about why I was hurting myself motivated me, but didn't solve the problem. After about six years, I'm still working on my denial around picking at my cuticles. I work at noticing the different conditions, and ways of touching my fingers, that have led to such picking, and I still fail sometimes. As with all attempts at change, the starting point is finding acceptance. Like addressing my obesity, I hadn't acknowledged that I had a problem with my cuticle picking.

The denial allowed the behavior to become deeply entrenched in my subconscious. When I decided I needed to change the behavior, I found that my denial was easy and frequent. One denial would protect another. Established behavior circuits in the brain respond to change like a bank denying your credit card when an unusual charge appears.

Asking ourselves why we have a bad habit can be helpful in motivating us to change the behavior, but it isn't enough. We must discover, root out, and develop an approach to addressing our denial. It doesn't matter how big a problem the obsessive behavior is (from just thinking, to issues like abuse of alcohol and sex). Behaviors can become compulsive, but behaviors originate in the brain, and the brain is where they can be controlled.

One of the first enemies to face is frustration when a problem seems to continue beating us. Numerous times I told myself to stop picking my cuticles, only to find myself picking again in seconds. Many people give up at that point. We get tired of the behavior making a fool of us. Accepting the embarrassment of having the problem just becomes easier.

ACCEPTANCE

The concern is that acceptance of embarrassing problems can be problematic. Instead of recognizing acceptance as the beginning of personal work to be addressed on a problem, it can be used as an excuse. We can always say to ourselves that people just don't understand how hard we've tried, which supports our denial. Perhaps people won't blame us for problems like alcoholism, but they won't necessarily respect us either.

Most of us know that everyone has problems. That's a good thing to know, but we're at risk if we use the idea to defend our denial. Does everyone having problems mean that our problems aren't serious? More likely, we're at risk of using our knowledge to trick ourselves into protecting a deep fear. Then it's easier not to do the hard work of personal change.

The work of personal change starts with not only acknowledging we have a problem, but also believing that we can stop it. When we're obese, we must question ourselves about issues like whether eating something sweet after dinner, even if we're full, is a compulsive behavior. Some may need to decide whether they're keeping their house too clean for the wrong reasons and missing out on something larger for their life. Others may need to notice that they drink more than what would be helpful for solving the problems that depress them. No matter what the issue, all of us need to know how to change our behaviors.

AVOIDING NEGATIVE JUDGMENTS

To address compulsive problems, we have to step out of our denial. We need to think about the negative judgments and labels we sometimes place on ourselves. We have to be patient to win success. One little piece of success may not do it for us, but successes that build on a success will help us be patient. Small successes and patience leads to believing in change.

An initial success might come when we notice that we're thinking about the problem and considering ways to address it. We don't necessarily have to figure out why we engage in a behavior, but we do need to pinpoint when we're likely to do it. I became very aware that I picked at my cuticles most during therapy sessions and at other stressful times.

I then found some success by either holding my hands apart or lacing my fingers together during times of possible stress. Because I had already learned patience and success while fighting my overeating issues, finding such a plan for this compulsive disorder was easier this time. Knowing that I was limiting the reinforcement of an old mental program while I developed new-program neural connections was also helpful. The more we address denial, the easier overcoming it becomes. Patience comes more easily, too, when we've had success and understand what we're doing.

We might compare the task of facing denial to running out of patience with a jigsaw puzzle when we don't have any techniques developed, and just aren't making any progress. We may have learned to look for edges and colors, but our sense of tabs and pockets hasn't been developed. Addressing denial is like finishing a puzzle. We need to choose a winnable task and stay with it until we win. It helps if you know other good puzzlers: people who have won some personal battle by staying aware of the multiple issues.

THE ROLE OF MISTAKES

It's rare to learn a new behavior without learning to notice our mistakes. Our errors don't always hurt us, but being aware of them is usually important for improving our behaviors. Trying to be perfect isn't a healthy idea, but learning to better ourselves is important for our happiness. Improvement supports self-esteem; self-esteem facilitates motivation for change.

Advances in neuropsychology have established that some of us will have less help from our brain regarding consequences. In a study of young men with multiple felonies, researchers found them to have greatly underdeveloped prefrontal cortical structures, the part of the brain where consequences are reviewed. These structures have been called the executive part of the brain, where we make decisions about thoughts and behaviors. We all approach denial in the same way, but people with such a disability will need to slow down, and take time for more thinking to find success.

LEARNING TO HOPE

For anyone to experience positive change in their lives, they must have reason to hope. Working for even the smallest of changes helps with this issue. Hopelessness feeds denial, and denial often supports hopelessness. Ironically, hopelessness is easily and commonly encouraged. Sympathy is far easier than support for struggle in most relationships. Honest appraisal, even among the closest of friends, often is lost in the face of denial and defensiveness.

Adding to the problem, physicians rarely have enough psychology to encourage behavior change beyond words that often discourage. The resulting failures with behavioral issues can then become a loss of hope. Further, those who are still negatively habituated, like those who still smoke cigarettes, tend to find support from others who have also given up. Studies also suggest that obese individuals influence each other negatively, probably due to support for their hopelessness.

The only thing we can do about hopelessness is develop false hope or make progress. Of course, the latter is the successful way. Progress is about feeling agency. Any progress will help as long as we don't label our denial-surrounded problem as impossible to fix. I love the story about the two frogs that fell in a deep hole. They jumped up, but the hole appeared to be too deep. Their friends looked at them and started screaming. One frog lay down and died while the other jumped and jumped and jumped. Finally the jumping frog's feet dug a slight perch from which he then was able to free himself with one more jump. When his friends asked where he gained such determination, he responded that he was rather deaf and thought they were yelling at him to keep trying.

If we don't give up, we can find value in honoring our feelings that we can do nothing about our circumstances. Awareness is the first step of change. Then we realize that losing hope is always a mistake and accept that there is usually something we can do about a condition. I don't mean that we'll be able to live when told we're about to die. I mean that getting stuck in negativity always makes things worse.

Even when death is said to be certain, we can make choices that will determine what our death will be like. When life is short, addressing our denial is all the more important. Most of us feel that dying alone is to be avoided if at all possible. If we've been a person known for being miserable, the need to change our attitude will be more dramatic when facing dying alone. Denial has likely supported this negative aspect of our personality. We've probably denied that we have opportunities to advance our social skill, and we probably despair at changing ourselves. However, it really isn't that difficult to at least avoid expressing our misery so often around those who care for us.

POSSIBILITY

The opposite of hopelessness is possibility. Humans have a lot of limitations, but we always have possibility if we aren't in denial about it. Behavioral problems are so often intransigent because we get caught up in compulsive negative thinking. The really good news is that we can always cease compulsive thinking. The hard news is that it takes work. It takes belief that we can change. Humans tend to be base-huggers, especially when we're distressed. We cling to status quo, even when it's terrible. Denial can keep us from seeing the possibility in our lives, and then failure becomes a compulsive cycle.

When we feel stupid or defeated, denial easily keeps us from trying anything new. We deny that we could succeed. We deny that we haven't worked hard or long enough. We need to recognize and stop such negative thoughts. We may have worked at it before and think that our thoughts can't be stopped, but we need to believe we can. Patience and progress build our hope for the steps we take that can change our destiny.

FEELING HELPLESS

Negative thinking is like a cup of poison. It might as well be. It's easy to become compulsive about thinking negatively. Consistent negativity develops helplessness and hopelessness. Hopelessness doesn't just cause us to miss an opportunity, but it can also literally kill our will to live, and eventually our bodies. Even when we don't believe we can change, risking the frustration of attempts that fail has more possibility than giving up. Then if we discover what we've been denying, if we find what to successfully work on, possibility has a chance in our lives.

Without the denial perspective, we have little positive expectation for behavior change related to compulsivity. We tend to see the negative behavior as having the power, when it's our denial that's powerfully affecting us. We don't need to find reasons for that, or blame anyone. We do need to see that such behaviors are quite stoppable. However, only when we approach them with understanding and hard work.

SUB-CLINICAL COMPULSIVITY

We all have issues of compulsivity. We call them habits when they don't rise to clinical importance. I was given a set of DVDs with *Monk* TV episodes. They feature a detective who is successful due to having an extreme case of obsessive-compulsive disorder. After getting over my initial judgment of repulsion to a program making fun of people with obsessive-compulsive disorder, I enjoyed the episodes. They ended up helping me notice just how compulsive I am. I recently noticed that a pot was not quite straight on the stove burner and, without thinking, reached out and straightened it. The move couldn't have made much of a difference in the heating of the pot. My wife and friends who know me well have teased me about such behaviors, but the behaviors don't rise to clinical importance, or require diagnosis. They would be more clinical if I chastised my wife for putting the pot on the stove crooked in the first place.

My experiences as a therapist led me to believe that many marital problems are simply such sub-clinical compulsive thinking or behavior that is taken too seriously. Knowing that some of my behaviors can be found humorous probably helped me relax and enjoy *Monk*, and certainly helped me further enjoy my wife and marriage. My compulsiveness makes many activities in my life easier. I usually know where the keys to the car are because I compulsively hang them up when I get home.

Is having a habit of hanging the keys up regularly a compulsivity problem? The behavior might be a problem if I believed it to be the only way to handle keys. I'm not in denial that people are different, have different habits, and don't mean to offend when the habits clash. We can gain nothing by denying, let alone being angry or judgmental, that people are all different when looked at closely.

WISDOM FROM ALCOHOLICS ANONYMOUS

For over 16 years, I attended Alcoholics Anonymous meetings to address my food issues and my cuticle picking. I had to find a small group willing to have a regular who wasn't an alcoholic. AA starts each meeting with a statement of acceptance: "I am an alcoholic." Sometimes people may claim that they're a "hopeless alcoholic," but hopefully they realize that is not reality, but rather a feeling. Acceptance is the necessary beginning point of all change. Then comes the work. The success of AA is based on people who share a similar struggle all helping each other.

An important piece that I learned at AA meetings was that those who say they're *trying* to quit rarely have success with compulsive behaviors. *Trying* can be used as an excuse, with an implication that success is unlikely. Rather, success is likely with work, partial successes, and the patience that grows with progress. We can't always immediately recognize the behaviors our unconscious mind is protecting, but we can stop denying and acknowledge the behavior we do notice, and identify any compulsivity in it. The unconscious near the surface of awareness is called our implicit memory. It is important to see what is implied in the behaviors that are continuing without our conscious permission.

For example, I suspect that a person who wasn't going to have desserts for a month, but quickly fails, might discover a thought such as, *Well, just this once.* Not discovered and acknowledged, the thought works. Denial has obscured such a person's awareness that thinking *just this once* has never worked. The statement is best seen as a bold lie. Not seen, the good intentions of trying to lose weight are defeated.

As well, a person who works her doctor for more of those pills—the ones she knows work best for her pain—knows that her hurt is deeper than any physical pain she may or may not have. Her denial is of awareness that she thinks she can't be happy without the drug. Such a thought is implied in her self-defeating behavior. With awareness, she could see that much could be done for her happiness.

CARELESS THOUGHTS

In learning about denial, I realized that I was in denial and convincing myself that I'd starve to death if I didn't plan for my next meal. The fact that my wife, before she feels hungry, could care less about when or what would be her next meal helped me to notice my denial about food: I realized the planning was about eating pleasure, not physical need. People suffering from alcoholism need to observe denial about planning to just drink a little, when it's likely the plan will lead to drinking more. When we accept that this thinking is denial, we may notice that drinking makes us feel good, but has consequences.

Without addressing denial and accepting our problem, for example drinking again, a thought such as, *I'd better not drink,* can easily also lead to drinking again. When we recognize such a behavior, we can realize that we're thinking about repeating a negative behavior when we make such statements.

Denying these types of thoughts and their implications can be deadly. It doesn't produce change. When these thoughts are obsessive, we need to stop them. Decades ago, psychologists developed thought-stopping techniques, some as simple as having a therapist shout, "Stop." Such a technique may work, if practiced over time, but there are many ways to stop obsessive thinking on your own.

Imagine whether you'd be thinking obsessively about something like food if someone were pointing a gun at you. Such a drastic thought can stop obsessive thinking that supports compulsivity. Pleasant thoughts, and even boring thoughts, like counting backwards, can work. If you recognize how some thought process has been leading to more of a problem behavior, you can easily come up with your own techniques.

We especially forget about the immediate value of pleasant thoughts. Remembering a pleasant river scene is even valuable in the dentist's chair. Pleasant thoughts can work so well we must be careful not to use them for denial. However, using them to break up a repeating thought about a piece of pie is an excellent strategy.

In addition to thought-stopping techniques, we also need to review the consequences of an undesirable behavior. Even tying troublesome thoughts to a noxious odor only works for a brief time, but staying aware of the damage our behaviors cause has a much longer effect. Thinking how awful death from obesity often is, before eating inappropriate foods, can be quite effective.

When we don't check our compulsivity, the first denial to notice is whether we're aware of suffering more consequences. Acceptance, again, is critical to relieving ourselves of more denial difficulties. With acceptance we can start noticing that we're denying that change can occur. We may already know ways to change, and there also may be techniques we haven't heard of yet.

ADDRESSING SHORTCOMINGS

We may have also denied that we're afraid of advice as it may force us to pinpoint our errors. A fear of addressing shortcomings can protect us from thoughts that we're not good enough. We usually have layer upon layer of denial behind our failures. Accepting that our failures are our responsibility, but not our fault, is always a good starting point. The next step is understanding denial enough to progress into accepting hope of change. Then hope, with experience, becomes belief: belief that we can be on the road to progress and happiness.

Digging deeper into the situations that can lead to our negative behaviors is critical for success. Researchers call this "relapse prevention," when we learn to recognize that we are thinking of drinking, for example, because we're hungry, angry, lonely, or tired (the HALT acronym used in AA). There are also social precursors to repeating known negative behaviors. The alcoholic is clearly in denial when he goes to a bar to buy some cigarettes.

Of course, in such times, we need to review the negative consequences. The first questions of a review need to be something like, *What is my history regarding the consequences for this behavior? Have I gone to the refrigerator before just to see what's available as though I won't eat anything?* Awareness of consequences can be effective with food in hand, but even better before the trip to the refrigerator.

It's likely we'll need to support our questions by checking if we're working hard at being honest with ourselves, or in denial. It's rare for a person with a drug problem to ask an untroubled person what he thinks the consequences of abuse will be. Again, we also have to notice, not deny, that we may be corrupting our view of the consequences by seeing them as the relief of hopelessness. When avoiding drinking, eating, or using, doesn't lead to quick and clear success, it doesn't compete well with the short-term result of using. Control of behaviors with negative consequences needs practice and maintenance.

Sadly, there is no simple one-size-fits-all solution to problems of denial. Our brains and their habit programs are greatly unique. Some generalization of approach can be made, but the rest is up to each individual. That's why behavioral suggestions made by friends and professional are so often useless, and frequently are taken as demeaning. Each of us needs to recognize our own tricky programs in support of old habits.

If we claim a negative compulsive behavior and want to focus on it, our focus must be on how and when we use denial. Not long ago, I ate a large, wonderful piece of cheesecake. I soon noticed that the taste wasn't worth what I figured to be about 3,000 mostly useless calories. My awareness came after years of work though.

After noticing this more work was useful. A review of consequences was helpful. My behavior of eating that cake felt like a potential step toward being obese again. Even if that felt like an exaggeration, a good denial defense, I questioned if I minded being still some 20 pounds overweight? Did eating the cheesecake feel like a setback, a temporary failure? My answers to such thoughts led to dropping cheesecake from the "must-have" category and into the "be careful" category.

I felt more success in returning to the same restaurant to eat lunch without a dessert. I was conscious of past failures and on guard for tricky thinking that had led to failures in the past. I had something to prove. I was putting my foot on the neck of an old habit. Though there was obviously some risk, I succeeded and enjoyed not having any dessert after a healthy lunch. If the result of a failure had been more dramatic, I wouldn't have taken the risk.

When we've unsuccessfully tried to control an obsessive problem, success from just thinking differently feels like a miracle. Most of us don't believe in miracles, which could be part of the problem. The hard part of behavior change is controlling the thinking, strengthening awareness, and overcoming denial. As an example, a friend has risked telling you she's worried about how much you drank at the last party. You hear yourself being defensive: You were just tired, excited, whatever.

Your friend is very brave and suggests that she's actually frequently worried about your drinking. This friend is quite willing to change the subject now, but she has you thinking. You realize you've thought about this drinking too much before and are amazed you haven't been noticing recently. You stopped drinking for a few weeks once, and started again thinking you'd have better control.

It's time to ask why you don't want to drink so much. That's a far better question than asking why you do at this point. Why you drink easily leads to guilt, whereas why it's a problem is more effective. Perhaps first in your mind is your friend's concern. That embarrasses you. Then there are issues like feeling out of control as you notice the progression of drinking more and more. Weight gain may be becoming a problem, and you remember briefly worrying about whether your liver is remaining healthy.

It is important to notice that the work is with yourself. You need to realize the fault is not on eating the cheesecake, drinking the alcohol, or engaging in whatever the behavior. Alcoholics have told me they didn't understand why anyone would drink one beer. I had probably told them I start feeling drunk with one and don't want any more. They sometimes told me they didn't even like beer, but that it was the least expensive way to achieve the feeling. That's an important realization for alcoholics. If they're addressing issues of denial, they may need to see that their problem is with feeling good, not with drinking.

We all want to feel good, and we all would like a good shortcut to feeling good. The problem is that such shortcuts aren't like paths that save time on a journey; they don't reach the destination, and often lead to bigger problems along the way. Fortunately, with awareness, shortcuts can sometimes be used to trigger the recognition of consequences.

One of my shortcuts for feeling better after overeating was using antacids. Probably from eating too fast and too much, I developed a digestive problem. Antacids worked for me, but I began taking more and more. I noticed that, when I ate more than usual, I needed more antacids. I was already thinking about eating less, so it was a fairly easy task to recognize acidity as a negative consequence. Eating less diminished my need for antacids.

When we're dealing with compulsive behaviors, we need to accept that shortcuts usually support denial. Drinking can be used as a shortcut to happiness. Cuticle picking, for me, was probably a shortcut to anxiety relief. Whatever the shortcut, denial clouds the issue or such behaviors would be given up quickly. Shortcuts have too many negative consequences.

When we're in denial, we may not think we have problems with happiness or anxiety. Shortcuts are often distractions, forms of denial in themselves. We worry about drinking too much, hurting our fingers, whatever, instead of concerning ourselves with a bigger issue that we need to deal with if we want to change.

If a "bigger issue" is killing us, it may amaze us to find we were more afraid of something like feeling we couldn't develop happiness in our lives.

When we recognize our denial, not facing issues like stress and unhappiness makes no sense. Even in despair it makes more sense to face problems, making new insights possible. Not facing problems leads to hopelessness and makes lapsing into useless shortcuts easier. If we don't avoid a problem like unhappiness, we will have the motivation that is often necessary to face such a worthy foe. Yes, unhappiness is a huge and complex problem. Often the ideas holding us back from making necessary change are imposters supported by denial.

Blaming others (for example a spouse) for our unhappiness is easy. Partnering can be both an expansion and a limitation in life. It's easy to focus on just the limitations. Feeling stuck in a partnership often leads to separations, but separations don't solve the problem. *I'll be darned; there are limitations in this new relationship as well. I thought this would be different.* Such declarations are common within a year or less of a new relationship. A relationship, or sex, or food doesn't bring happiness; progress made in all aspects of our personal lives does. When we can't progress in a relationship, we likely need to progress more as individuals if we want to find happiness and escape choosing compulsivity.

Money, partners, houses, cars, and food, can all be symbols of a type of success, but they aren't symbols of happiness. I don't think much happiness comes for free.

It's purchased with work. Yes, I was very happy eating that great piece of cheesecake, for a few minutes. Then I thought, *What have I done to myself?* A person with a drug addiction once told me that shooting cocaine made him happy for about 20 seconds. Then he was peeking out his window looking for cops for an hour.

Those of us with addictions presumably know no happiness beyond those few moments of the high. Without the distraction of a shortcut, we could be finding ways of being happy. Personal misery is usually programmed early in life, and well practiced. It's particularly tragic if we think of it as terminal. It takes mental work, but happiness is available to all.

We have to ask ourselves what we're doing wrong. Yes, this assumes personal responsibility, but addressing what we're doing wrong makes us aware of the only behavior we can fix. It doesn't work to be judgmental about our mistakes. Finding mistakes we're making is the work of developing in life. Finding mistakes can result in success, stepping toward enduring happiness.

We often learn to be judgmental early on. It's a problem of not training children in critical thinking. After we stop fighting our parents over toileting and eating habits, we tend to accept their behaviors and attitudes without weighing alternatives. Often teenage rebellion only temporarily relieves the problem in that the advice of peers is usually uninformed and ineffective. Lessons without critical thinking result in defensiveness; The other guy is wrong. Then we've learned to be judgmental.

As we discussed in the last chapter, critical thinking is what humans use to make positive changes in their lives. It's our way to avoid buying into the status quo. Blind acceptance of what others think requires protection from denial. The current use of salt in foods is a clear example. It isn't uncommon to hear about the dangers of too much salt in our food, but it seems like everyone does it. Critical thinking can lead to learning to enjoy tastes that are less salty. Critical thinking can also help with issues like noticing that people aren't at their social best when they drink too much.

When we don't deny known and unknown errors, we find that we really have a lot to learn if we value life. Our denial, that of those around us, and many general attitudes of society, all work against happiness. We live in a world where people rarely admit seriously that we all have problems to one degree or another. Perfect people really don't exist anywhere, and pretending to be all right inhibits growth. It's denial and it limits happiness.

Acceptance of the complexity of our problems is the only way to change them. For example, if we generally feel untrusting, we're probably looking at the tip of an iceberg in life. To start, we probably weren't taught skills related to trust as a child. Trust is a complex issue, which can encourage denial. Both too much trust and too little trust facilitates pain, even despair.

We need to learn that trustworthiness must be established before taking any sizable risk with others, but that not learning to trust anyone severely diminishes happiness. Judgmental labels, usually holistic, easily prevent even considering change and exacerbate problems like lacking trust. We tend to say of ourselves that we aren't able to trust. Then why bother? We might as well adjust to our unhappiness. Adjusting to trusting too much can have more dramatic consequences.

Ironically, the judgmentalism that we often learned from parents who didn't understand the importance of critical thinking limited our ability to make judgments about people's attitudes and behaviors. If we trust without making judgments about people and situations, we are likely to learn not to trust. Both personality and circumstances limit human trustworthiness. If we can't discriminate whom among our associates will take advantage of us at times, and who will be consistently balanced in the give and take of relationships, we may be hurt, angry, even judgmental.

If our parents weren't trustworthy, we may never try trusting the broader world as we enter it, no matter how much we learn about trust. Such limitations, especially when denied, lead to finding shortcuts and other avoidances. Awareness in relationships provides expansion while denial restricts progress, and can lead to compulsive behaviors.

Compulsivity then shrouds our limitations and their consequences by becoming the problem of choice. We can then have an alcohol problem or whatnot for distraction from our problem with happiness. Again, the plot thickens as we now have to deny the negative consequences of a compulsive behavior, or we'll be turned back to avoidance of our initial denial: our difficulty trusting enough to lead a full life with friends and accomplishments, for example.

When we free ourselves of denial, we are able to open our eyes and see that maintaining what we deem as status quo isn't a solution. Status quo is a place to hide, not a solution. Denial is a veil, not a brick wall. Sometimes we can lift the veil briefly, but we still have a lot of work to do. This work probably sounds tedious. Every time we fix one problem we're able to see more of them. That might seem depressing if it wasn't for the joy in knowing we're able to change, and the long-term rewards of the changes we make.

Feeling mellow by behaviors like drinking won't be important if we've done our denial work, and when drinking isn't important, our compulsivity ceases to exist. When we've noticed that picking at our cuticles is about being stressed, then we're far more likely to learn that we can lower our stress by changing our thinking and behaviors. I had to notice that I felt too responsible for my client's solutions. That wasn't good for either of us. I also needed to reduce my hours of work and adjust my budget.

It may amaze us how mellow we feel if we adequately address denial, because we will have made adjustments that will allow us to sit by a pond just watching some ducks, and not obsessing about having a drink. We will be able to see even negative compulsive behaviors as our friends. They hint to us that we need to wake up, realize that our living skills can be improved, and that we need to get to work.

Compulsive behaviors can help us to know that we not only aren't alone, we're sharing everyone's limitation. We are human, and it's wonderful to be human. When we pretend to be perfect, we're being defensive and we're misleading our friends and neighbors. Most of our fears and defenses have to do with being in denial about what it means to be humans.

STEPS THAT MAY DEEPEN UNDERSTANDING

1. Consider when you're compulsivity is negative. Have you given up changing a behavior that is worrying you or even causing your immediate trouble?

2. Does compulsivity hinder your life more than it helps? Do you have any behavior like my cuticle picking that provides some temporary relief, but has more lasting problem effects?

3. Practice not allowing a negative compulsivity for brief times.

4. Analyze whether compulsivity is an issue of personal security or of efficiency.

5. Choose what to be compulsive about. For example, if you often don't make your bed for the day, try making it every day as soon as you get up in order to notice how habits are developed.

Such sweet compulsion
doth in music lie.

John Milton

Chapter Four
ACCEPTANCE

Facing our denial is a complex task. Before effectively dealing with specific issues, like the problems I had with food, we have to think about the role of acceptance. Acceptance requires knowing that something is negative, wasn't intentional, needs to be dealt with if not completely changed, and will usually require patience and persistence.

As proponents for Dialectical Behavioral Therapy (DBT) have emphasized, acceptance is the ying and change is the yang in the circle of progress. We need both acceptance and change to be successful. Acceptance without effort for change is a mistake that may lead us to despair. Trying to make changes in our lives without acceptance may even be damaging. We would most likely be just avoiding change with short-sided temporary solutions, or defending ourselves and blaming others.

Problems are always supported by an issue that requires more understanding and acceptance. Recognizing avoidance of a problem should alert us to denial's ability to obscure. Questions need to be raised: Are we pretending they aren't problems? Are we afraid there aren't solutions?

When we start noticing denial in our lives, we can easily be overcome by a need for change, or to display agency, our ability to act. Humans don't do well without feeling agency. In denial, we easily become frozen and helpless. Feeling powerless, we tend to work on our defenses instead of our progresses. In learning to enjoy progress, we don't have to stress on goals. And goals won't frustrate us when we find they don't amount to what we expected.

When we deny the need for change, the issue of acceptance is likely the problem. When we don't feel acceptance, our approach is judgmental, and feeling judged leads us to either dig in our heels in a tug-of-war or to feel hopeless. Once I fully realized that I was obese, my next step was to accept my responsibility for the problem. Blaming my parents or corporations would have only lead to frustration. Blaming myself would have been even worse. Accepting my mistakes in thinking and behavior was found to be effective. Then, progress gave me hope.

It takes hope to change when we can't be forced some way. There are many techniques of forced change, and I know of none that work over time. Diets are a good example of forceful techniques of change that are known not to work; they're just another short-cut. New diets still gain brief popularity, but that is likely due to hopeless desperation. I doubt that anyone chooses to die slowly from obesity. Even when those who are obese are physically still fairly healthy, they suffer from limitations. They also often face vicious judgmental observations, and may suffer emotional issues, from defensiveness to despair.

For those dealing with obesity, for example, the first step against denial of such a critical problem is acceptance that we are obese. The next step is often to accept that we feel powerless over the obesity. Our parents may have been obese. Often our friends are obese. No one seems to win against the problem. Then, in the step so often obscured by denial, we need to notice any mistakes we make regarding eating and exercise. We can catch ourselves feeling deprived if we can't have fats and sweets, or as much food as we think we want.

With acceptance, we can determine the choices we are making. We aren't depriving ourselves of anything good over the long run. Denial is what deprives us of our health and happiness when we're obese. We can accept that food isn't the enemy, but denial is. We can accept that healthy choices are opportunity, not restriction.

Denial, the opposite of acceptance, is the method of choice for many to remain unaware of a problem like obesity. We deny that we eat too much and exercise too little. We let feelings of hopelessness blur acceptance of our mistakes. The practice of war is similar in that it is usually sold as a necessary force, something we can't control. Governments easily lead people into feeling powerless over war. If war has ever accomplished positive change, it is far overshadowed by negative consequences, but we usually deny such issues as being too painful.

We're not talking about accepting one's plight in life. This acceptance is about taking responsibility for your plight, and finding something you can do about it. Thus, there is judgment of the issue as negative, but not of the person who is facing the problem. Making such a judgment is acceptance. Now we're ready for change. Now we're ready to discover levels of denial that we may not have realized we'd learned.

LEARNING ABOUT HABITS

Ever since we learned to tie our shoes, we might have noticed that we form habits fairly easily. Habits feel good when we choose them. The problem is that many of our habits aren't consciously chosen. I split the difference on the height of a bathroom mirror with my wife for years, and learned to bend over to comb my hair. Now I have a taller mirror and still bend over to comb my hair unless I catch myself. Noticing that a habit is engrained, unconscious, and a negative in your life is the beginning of acceptance.

When we can accept a negative habit, we can change it. Many people don't believe this because they've tried an ineffective approach to change. They've berated themselves, made promises, tried substitutes, kept charts, punished themselves, and much more. Some of these approaches work for a time, but all usually fall short of stable success. You can substitute extreme exercise for healthy food choices, but you're still damaging your body, and age often makes weight gain more dramatic.

Once we accept a personal problem, we need patience because it's likely that supporting habits are deeply engrained. However, patience becomes easier when we make obvious progress. Compare that to what happens when pressure fails: Negative labels, impatience, and lack of positive expectation. When we consider ourselves stupid, we don't expect to suddenly do better next time. Those who learn acceptance are wise people with some bad habits on which they're making progress.

A bad habit can be as subtle as thinking we're no good at math, a double-edged sword in that we then are unlikely to learn differently about our skill. Such thinking is a denial habit. We've accepted a problem in a negative way. We get out of trying with such acceptance, but we also limit our range of possibilities. Math is a highly useful language of numbers. Languages are all overly difficult if we don't learn some basics like grammatical rules and vocabulary. I thought I was language-challenged until I figured out that learning a language takes time.

Just as learning to do subtraction requires knowing the rules, breaking bad habits requires knowing the rules for acceptance and resisting our denial. The rules for this science of life are many, but acceptance, not denying, is a critical one. We must be cautious about feeling certain about anything. This troubles many scientists, and the ones who know the most often have the most difficulty.

THE RULE OF ACCEPTANCE

Certainty and its colleague arrogance are clues for using the rule of acceptance. Even if we must accept something that can't be changed, such as a malformed body, it is a subtle form of arrogance to assume we can do nothing about it. Accepting a limitation is different from accepting a mistake that we can change, but we need this critical rule of acceptance in both forms.

Acceptance includes knowing that no one is anywhere near perfect. Accepting is acknowledging that we won't have time to fix all of our known problems. And we'll also need to accept new problems that are sure to be discovered over time if we aren't too deeply into denial. Accepting involves knowing that there will always be people better at certain behaviors than we are and that, when it appears that we're the best at something, the feeling might not last long.

Let's consider these matters, and see if we can find beauty in it all. Even if we've intellectually known that this is the nature of human beings, accepting involves applying this information to ourselves. There's power in such knowledge. Once we feel like winners, like people who can change and grow, having more to do will be a positive. People literally die when they give up on growth. Life has to have meaning or we don't survive even when death doesn't take us.

Acceptance is a matter of perspective. How do we see our potential, our problems? Where denial obscures such issues, acceptance allows us to focus on them. Some people see themselves as too old to start writing books. Some of us still start writing. Some are stopped by knowing how difficult publishing is. Some of us still try. We've accepted the difficulty and accepted that we want to say something to a broad audience. Such an attitude is a perspective that is open to thinking about both positive and negative possibilities. This is the opposite of hiding in denial.

Often when despair is the result at the end of a successful career, success from that career may have been bought with some luck, work that was obviously paying off, and possibly even fun. When the body ages or the rules change, we have to understand the issue of continuing growth, that change requires acceptance. Wishing for things to be different can lead us down the road to despair, or of acceptance of needed changes. When people hold rigidly to a goal, they may be denying their humanity: the reality of failure and change. When we accept changes in ourselves, we can see that life demands that we be flexible.

PROTECTING ACCEPTANCE

Even if I hadn't experienced a few tragedies of my own, I could certainly notice them in the news. Bad things happen. Learning this can be devastating. But not denying the bad news of life can lead to acceptance, being more ready, and living free from fear. When we know bad things can happen, we can also consider each situation. Fearing events over which we have no control is a waste of time. And denying our behaviors that lead to negative events is a waste of life.

At my age, I occasionally consider losing people and activities that I enjoy. I'm aware that cell-phone-using drivers, like drunk drivers, randomly kill, and that keeping my health in this contaminated world isn't entirely up to me. Such rationalizing doesn't change how much a major change in one's life hurts, but it does help me continue with my life. I don't know what I would do if my wife died before me, but I know that I plan to go on. Working on my independence is a good skill. I'll be able to clean and cook if she dies. Not being able to use a computer is a frightening thought for me as well, but ALS only slowed Stephen Hawking; it didn't stop him.

I often experience that my acceptance of myself and of others is fragile and needs to be protected with awareness. When I wasn't accepting of how intelligent and well educated I am, I bragged and intimidated people. Claiming to be intelligent is itself usually considered to be bragging. It is bragging when it's judgmental, when it compares people instead of intelligence.

When I wasn't accepting of this factor, I was insecure and constantly trying to prove how smart I was. One of my psychology professors took me aside and told me that I was intimidating. He suggested that if I would accept I was intelligent and well educated, others would find relating to me easier. He was right of course.

The insight helped with a significant change in my life. After writing papers that were over 100 pages at Yale, and "short" papers at Wesleyan that were 20 pages, I was hostile and intimidating with students in colleges, where I occasionally taught, when they choked on requirements for a six-to eight-page paper. I now accept that my education was privileged, not available for most students, and wouldn't be the best experience for everyone. Such progress isn't available in denial; it requires acceptance.

EMBRACING PROBLEMS

Whereas we block awareness of a problem when in denial, we embrace problems when in acceptance. When we have been too protected by parents, busyness, food, or drugs, we may find it hard to imagine that embracing problems can be a good thing. Yes, if we ignore our problems and they pile up, as they usually do, we may need to be careful about becoming overwhelmed. Accepting that avoidance has been a mistake can be the safest starting point.

Our first task will be to avoid self-judgment. Did we choose our parents? Our early environment? These early factors all influenced the choices we've made.

Acceptance as embracing is a matter of just holding on to the idea of the mistake. We are not the mistake, but it is not wise to put knowledge of it behind us either. We actually need to watch for the reappearance of familiar mistakes.

Like anything we hold very long, we will find that holding our awareness of mistakes too long can be heavy. We'll have to put them down, yet picking them up regularly will be important for discovering change in our lives. We'll also need to remember that there is no value in blaming our parents, because we'd have to blame their parents, and their parents. Embraced as an entity different from us, though important to us, our mistakes can become friends.

The world seems to be lacking in acceptance, yet full of blame and other judgmentalism. In the mental health field, the push for diagnosis may have been helpful for research and insurance purposes, but it facilitated the worst of judgmentalism. How do you say that someone is mentally challenged without suggesting that the rest of us aren't? If some have trouble with emotional regulation and behaviors, are the diagnosticians always in control of themselves? The issue is usually one of degree, not of essential difference.

Acceptance is embracing ourselves and can lead to acceptance of even our most frightening mistakes. When we accept ourselves with patience, we develop the skill of accepting others, without feeling powerless. This act of acceptance is so common to both personal and larger issues that progress can be made in both areas at the same time. Individuals not caught in denial consistently make positive changes in their lives.

ADJUSTING TO REALITY

Progress itself requires acceptance. Those who appear to feel safer in the status quo are likely to be found in denial. Our world changes so rapidly that it's even difficult to finish any growth, as more is usually needed quickly. And growth tends to open our eyes to more reality. If we're not fearfully hanging onto our status quo, change may fascinate us. There is no end to it.

Acceptance doesn't just apply to big issues. It's needed just to cut a board. We need to know that the board could move. A saw or splinter could hurt us. We might find that the cut board doesn't fit like we thought, or we might even have cut it inaccurately. When we accept these and other possibilities, we are far more likely to cut the board well and safely. And, we can easily try again or change direction. Without acceptance, we are likely to become defensive, blaming the saw or claiming we didn't want the product anyway. There is no progress in such attitudes.

These attitudes are called defenses and are significant deterrents to acceptance. Rigid self-assuredness and arrogance are common clues that we are afraid to embrace some information. At times, it may seem that we're just afraid that the information might be out there. Yes, humans can usually do better, but it means facing that we're making mistakes.

Parenting is one of the areas where information can be frightening. People who've been parents know they make mistakes unless they're in complete denial. Fearing that it's our fault our children aren't successful is a waste of our lives. When we are willing to notice our failures as a parent, our sadness is far healthier than the anxiety of taking blame for the effects of our mistakes. Sadness is a clear emotion, can be free of blame, and tends not to lead to further mistakes like trying to solve the problems of our adult children.

I recognized a mistake I made when I emotionally disappeared during my divorce. My sons have benefitted from my acknowledgement that things weren't right with me. They've been more able to embrace their own shortcomings, and have more than an image of a father in their lives. I also think that any maturity in my relationships with my sons is a good model for their relationships with family and others.

Most of our defenses arise from a lack of confidence that we will be able to handle the unknowns of life. These defenses are very limiting and require a great deal of denial. Holding on to them is a little like hiding in a bunker after our side has lost a war. It takes no responsible choices to let life's events take us out. If you've ever known a serious addict, you know how little threat it takes for them to want a fix. They are like small children without parents to protect them from the dangers of life.

HUMAN POTENTIAL

Possibility is at the core of acceptance problems, and comparison exacerbates them. The potential of humans is incredible, and each of us develops in individual ways. If you start playing the cello as an adult, you have to accept that it isn't likely that you're going to be a Yo-Yo Ma who started at four. It amazes us to watch the Cirque du Soleil performers, as they are so skilled with their bodies that we usually don't even try to compare. We get defensive when someone more at our level is better than us in some specific way. Through acceptance, we can take pleasure in our ability to grow and acknowledge that many differences are about circumstance.

The possibilities of our lives can be an acceptance problem itself. It can be difficult to embrace knowing that effort makes many accomplishments available. So much is possible it can be confusing, even frightening. We need to accept not just what's possible, but whether we want to make the time for some accomplishment. I've actually found myself enjoying the fact that I have less time left in my life for some of the things I've considered doing.

Though I doubt that I could catch up to my wife's skill level, I could learn to ride horses, but I wouldn't have time to write. Denial at such a point, driven usually by some emotional need, could easily lead to frustration, even despair. Acceptance leads to a sense of fulfilment even though all of one's possibilities are far from accomplished. I was going to build a sailboat, but now don't think there's time even to learn how. It feels all right. I like what I'm doing more than what I might be doing.

Acceptance involves appreciating ourselves. This can be taken as satisfaction, but we need to be careful about being satisfied with our condition. Being satisfied with our progress is a whole different issue. As I have learned to accept myself, I've found that making progress is a critical aspect of my happiness.

I'm actively unhappy with the human condition in general. I find it so bad that I couldn't look at it if I hadn't found happiness in my personal progress. Greed, deception, and a lack of caring about people and the earth can easily depress me. As I write, the affluent of the world appear to think of the economically challenged like armies think of their enemies.

To stay happy, I've had to learn to tolerate that which is left unfinished. I didn't understand this issue most of my life. I still take pleasure in finishing something, but I now know that nothing human is ever really finished. Working with human lives as a psychologist left me frustrated at times, especially due to my honoring of individuality. However, I don't think forcing an individual into seeing things the way someone else thinks is best can be considered a healthly activity. I don't care how much training and experience a counselor may have, advice is usually demeaning where discovery is exciting.

I used to claim that I liked weeding the rows of carrots in our garden because I could finish the job.

I did notice that the weeds quickly came back, but that was just another task that could be finished. Accepting the persistence of weeds was important. I might have given up what I enjoy about gardening. You can address personality issues in a similar way, with pleasure knowing that more awaits you. Failure has to do with bringing pressure on ourselves. Even when the pressure appears to be coming from someone else, you are actually the one applying it. Pressure may be a sign that you're not employing acceptance.

THE ROLE OF TRUST

Trust is closely related to acceptance. If you trust that making progress at your own pace will get you to a good place, you'll be happy getting there. I'm not thin yet, and I keep making obvious eating mistakes, but my success helps me trust that making progress is enough. I do have a goal, but it's a direction, not an accomplishment. It isn't even about weight at this point; it's about improving agency, gaining more control over my food issues.

When you can accept that you have a problem that you've recognized as impeding you in an important way, the next step is to accept your limitations. Just your physique may make your goal impossible. However, it will be important not to accept physical limitations too quickly. I love the story of Spud Webb being one of the shortest men in the NBA. He loved the game, practiced all the time, even as a child, and is said to have learned to jump 42 inches high. That made him almost ten feet tall. He embraced his limitations, and found a way around them.

Accepting our limitations is often the easy part. Seeing a way around them is more difficult, physically and emotionally. Sometimes nothing can be done about a personal limitation. Even then, acceptance is critical for developing our lives. We all have limitations. Even if we have to accept progress only in other areas of our lives, being familiar with the limitation keeps it from discouraging us in our other objectives.

Sometimes getting help with limitations is necessary. Then care must be taken that the help is our choice so we take pride in our decision and don't feel demeaned by needing help. Sometimes help is mechanical, but often it is by way of a helper. Helpers come fraught with potential negatives that often must be accepted if the help is to be valued. Many helpers may guide us too much when what we need is knowledge of how to do something. The best helpers support improved thinking about a troubling issue. These best helpers sometimes find that they get no credit for remarkable change.

I heard that two psychologists raised a child with Down Syndrome who obtained a college degree with six years of effort. That may have been satisfying to all concerned, but acceptance of possible denial of emotional issues, and of alternative consequences, need to be closely considered. If such an education of a neurologically challenged person just led to a fuller life, all is well. If it led to bragging rights, true success is far less likely. It would have, for instance, been quite easy to make this child dependent on her parents for feeling able to be successful.

The issue is about balancing happiness. Denial is easily at play when we enjoy our accomplishments without full acceptance of all the consequences. Not everything that makes us feel accomplished also makes us experience more happiness in the future. An early hurdle in this game of life can frequently be not simply enjoying previous accomplishments. Ego often supports denial and is perhaps the largest limiting factor that must be understood and accepted.

I was quite proud of my grades in high school, but in denial about not seriously studying. My academic life was too easy until I entered a college. I almost flunked out my freshman year. Without acceptance of the problem, I put a lot of pressure on myself, which just caused anxiety and made me wonder if my mind even worked. I complained to a dean that I could make myself sit at a desk, but couldn't make myself study. My naïve-about-college parents had given me confidence in myself somehow, so I hung in and graduated with a C+ average. To do even that, I had to accept that I didn't know how to study.

In graduate school, I firmed up my new understanding when faced with learning the Greek language. I studied three hours a day for this course and earned an "A." I confirmed that intelligence wasn't enough, that learning frequently required work. I had accepted that something I didn't know about life was in the way of something I wanted to accomplish. Fortunately, I didn't have to understand that I'd learned to give up without trying. I just had to accept that serious academic learning requires a strong work ethic, and that I needed one.

Without this acceptance, I might have blamed the college, my high school, my parents, or God (if I was desperate). Acceptance is always within us. It is easier if it's just about us, not about comparing ourselves to others. In that we don't develop consistent rational thinking until we're about 14, I had little control over who I was when I got to college. My strengths and weaknesses, and everything in between, were imposed and developed without my rational consent. I now see a picture in my mind of the day I stepped on a train for the East Coast. Through the luck of a big scholarship, I was on my way into independent thinking and becoming responsible for myself.

TAKING RESPONSIBILIY

Looking back, much of it feels like luck, but I feel that my acceptance of problems has played a large role in my development. I'm not known as a person who looks back, or celebrates the "good ol' days," but when I consider my life, I feel good about it. That doesn't mean I haven't had some amends to make, and some I couldn't make. It doesn't mean there haven't been some deep pains, but all has felt like a gift once embraced. I've reached a good level of happiness and wouldn't be here without my past. By taking responsibility to accept the good and the bad in me, I started appreciating the negativity of denial in my life.

I've told a biblical story to more than a few clients who suffered trauma. It's about a man who was attacked by a spirit, and they wrestled for a long time. The spirit broke the man's thigh with a touch, but the man continued to fight. The spirit asked the man what it would take for him to quit fighting. The man responded that he would have to be blessed by the spirit. The stubborn fighter was greatly blessed.

And so it is with the struggle of life. Accept it, embrace the pains, and be blessed. I think this is what J. Krishnamurti was getting at when he was purported to say about his own happiness during a talk in the later part of his life: "This is my secret. I don't mind what happens," (reported in *A New Earth,* by Eckhart Tolle, Penguin Group, New York, 2006, p. 198). Acceptance expands the possibilities of our lives and, by assisting progress, brings us happiness.

STEPS THAT MAY DEEPEN UNDERSTANDINNG.

1. Consider the continuum from acceptance to denial. Are you, for example, accepting of your body image, but in denial about being overweight? Are you accepting that you have compulsive

behaviors, but in denial that some are hazardous to your health?

2. Evaluate your approach to self-appraisal.

3. Reflect on how open you are to advice, even when you've asked for it. Do you ever get defensive? Are you able to hear and consider such advice?

4. Notice when you get defensive.

5. Do you have problems with follow-through on change when you have a negative self-appraisal?

If you can't see the past
you can't see the future.

Stuart Ewen

CHAPTER FIVE
FEAR

In understanding that denial can be avoidance of intolerable thoughts, both conscious and unconscious, we can see that fear is primarily responsible for much of a person's denial. Further troubling, what frightens us, and how we handle it, is often well in place before the end of childhood. Our childhood fears don't go away when we don't develop effective ways to deal with them, and fearfulness can get worse as we mature. When fear is incapacitating, a person often seeks professional help, but when the fears are just part of an underlying attitude, we often allow them to shrink our life's capacity. Then negative uses of denial are given free reign to limit our maturation, and can even hasten our death.

In understanding denial, we need to know that we often share at least some of the fears of our parents, and we often don't learn better ways of facing them. Then again, dealing with our own frightening experiences often demands more skills than we've acquired. A lot of things go bump in the nights of our lives, creating fears and experiences we need to learn to handle. There are few experiences that sometimes aren't feared: love, sex, happiness, money, comes to mind, but even these are feared at times.

Fear of memories, and not just trauma memories, can be huge. Even memories of thoughts can frighten us. Such thoughts can be anything from suicide to buying a chocolate bar. Denial of anything out of fear isn't healthy. Take the thought of a chocolate bar. Let's say that this fear is derived from knowing we have a compulsion for chocolate that we've seen to be significant problem in our life. It isn't a life or death issue, but it has been seriously frustrating. Not noticing a flash of fear about eating chocolate is almost a guarantee of failure of intention.

Some thoughts are more immediately significant. Fearing thoughts of taking our own life are especially dangerous to deny. It can lead to not being ready to find alternatives to a final denial of our lives. Fearing trauma memories denies our chances of finding control of them, and of noticing their negative effects in our lives.

Let's say we fear a thought because it has always led to having another failure. We've eaten the chocolate bar, attempted suicide, or gotten caught up in trauma memories instead of controlling them. It's difficult to break such a negative cycle. Negative labels can then dominate us, and help us deny that there is anything new that can be done.

Trapped in negativity, it's often best to find help, but we can think our way out of it without help as well. It will be most important to notice that letting fear put us into denial sets us up to fail again. Denial at such a time just delays our next experience of failure. Denying the fear makes it all right to have the chocolate, and likely more than we might otherwise have eaten. Of more immediate significance, such denial can make suicide feel all right.

An effective response to such thoughts is to acknowledge them and go further into the consequences of our compulsion. Does chocolate taste as sweet as losing weight? Have I had any success in the past, and does it feel good? Have friends told me they see more in me than I do? Have I tried many solutions for my despair? Would it be much of a risk to try thinking positively about myself for even a few weeks?

The risk taking we usually fear has to do with hope and despair. When hope has too often led to failure and despair, we easily fear trying to hope again. And if we experience despair as uncontrollable, we fear noticing such an experience. Unnoticed, these fears control our attempts at changing our lives.

Not understanding this general aspect of denial can be fatal—slowly fatal perhaps—by continuing behaviors risky to health, and more assuredly fatal through serious depression. Suicides can often have an accidental quality due to denial. Those who've survived jumping off of high places have sometimes revealed that they changed their mind too late to reach back to safety. Others, not in denial, who just think about killing themselves often end up finding a better solution to their pain.

The thoughts most feared are usually those of trauma memories. They are experienced like Br'ere Rabbit's tar baby: Touch them and we can become stuck. But untouched and denied, the fright generalizes to all of the shadows of life. Several approaches to psychotherapy teach such clients to touch and release, distract, and move on to rationalizing about the situation. Yes, more ugly events might come up in a life, but only if we're living. Those who've experienced trauma know well that bad things happen within the overall beauty of life. Remembering the beautiful part is important to survival, but easily denied if we're stuck in trauma emotions.

One of my friends has had several major traumas in her life. Yes, she still can start a day with anxiety, but quickly claims victory over it. More importantly, she doesn't add to her fears. She has mostly good days and, with them, comes a feeling of accomplishment. Facing past and potentially ugly events in our lives takes courage, but it gets easier as we claim our powers of control.

Human life is an insignificant part of the history of the earth, but terribly significant if it's our life. We can do a great deal to increase safety in living, but we can't control everything. When we're not in denial, we can be happy with an amount of control and find escaping general fearfulness to be enough. Some of us mistake perfectionism for control, but it doesn't take long to find that we aren't God. We don't want our emotions or our lives to be out of control, but neither do we want them over controlled, or overprotected by naïve denial thinking.

Not being overly fearful helps us keep the balance; too much fear supports denial that life is both not charmed and not always tragic. Surely a place where everyone loves each other wouldn't be very interesting. But life is unliveable if it's just tragic expectation. If our personal philosophy of life is basically negative, denying the effects of self-destructive behaviors like addictions becomes easy.

On the other hand, an overly optimistic view of life, and its denial of potential failure, can lead not only to failures, but can also inhibit growth and wisdom. Trouble is often our first educator. Overcoming denial of things that should be worrisome, if not frightening, can lead to more safety, maturity, and happiness.

MANY CONSEQUENCES TO FEAR

Along with fears we learn from our parents, we can also learn fears by being afraid of our parents. Parents in the United States are still mostly punitive in their child-raising practices. Punishment does terrible things to self-esteem. Punishment often teaches children that they are wilfully stupid or bad, and that they can't count on the consistent support of their primary caregivers.

If we were often afraid of our parents, we can easily treat all authorities, and new ideas, like the parents we feared. It's as if we fear being called stupid or bad in some way. The more a person is in denial about such situations, the worse off they are. It would be certainly rare for us to fix a problem when we are keeping ourselves unaware.

We have many ways to react to such hidden fears, but their protectors, avoidance and defensiveness, are rigid and not very adaptable. We can use incredible excuses like calling ourselves stupid, which seems to help in the short run. Only when we stop denying that we have problems, can we discover the unconscious fears impeding our lives.

Problems can get old, but they rarely fade away. They are even frequently reborn in combination with other problems, new and old. We may start out denying something, like being afraid that we aren't as smart as most people. That can leave us either bluffing, with all of the insecurity and embarrassment that goes with that, or not trying. When we're afraid of trying new behaviors, we risk being teased about our reticence. This, again, can lead to avoiding people we don't know to be safe.

When we allow our perceived limitations of life to pile up, it's easy to end up hidden away with a small circle of co-dependent friends. Being fearful of recognizing what our life is truly like can compound this. Pretending to enjoy living is not as healthy as knowing we aren't happy. Denial by pretending can be an unnecessary stressor, and can limit our recognition of solutions. This, too, can all start when we're very young.

PERSONALITY

One of the most important places where fear of changing a status quo can be extremely limiting is with regard to our personalities. Styles of personality are greatly shaped by how we were attended to in our first year of life. The style of attachment that an infant learns starts with genetics and is firmly established in the first year of parenting. Such styles influence relationships and range from being withdrawn, to feeling anxious, or to being secure. Chromosomes establish how we start these styles, but the behaviors can be significantly modified by the relationship children have with their primary caregiver. This pattern easily becomes the approach used with other people and to new events in general. And it is a significant area where denial can limit us.

These styles of relationship to new people and things normally lasts a lifetime. Most psychologists currently believe that such patterns can be modified if they're brought to a person's awareness. Often, primary caregivers have no idea how powerful the attention or lack of attention that they give to infants will be in forming this important aspect of the child's personality.

Caregivers may treat children in a similar style of relationship that they experienced in their infancy due to not perceiving how their treatment as an infant led to their own problems. Sometimes the issue is more due to infants being neglected because caregivers have become distracted by other severe issues in their own lives.

Those who have withdrawn styles of attachment probably carry the most fear and obvious social inhibition. However, those with anxious and ambivalent styles just have a different form of social limitation. They often have an exaggerated need for attachment that leads to feeling uncomfortable in relationships. That can be challenging to the relationship. Life is remarkably fuller for those with a secure attachment style. They tend to have less denial, but they do need to be careful about overconfidence. Those who feel secure have the same limitations as everyone else regarding skills, luck, and awareness; they still need to work at life.

DEALING WITH FEARFULLNESS

Wherever they came from, most of the fears that limit new behaviors and experiences are related to unknown consequences. Early in our lives, we had very few known consequences. We quickly added such lessons, which were both positive and negative. If our experiences were more positive than negative, we experienced less fear about unknown consequences than those whose experiences were unbalanced negatively.

Those of us with less fear may take more risks, learn more, and expand our lives if we're not in denial about levels of dangerousness. Those with more fear about the unknown tend to use denial more and are greatly limited to what they already know. In a changing world, such a limitation can be devastating. Some third-generation autoworkers in Detroit, for example, may wish they hadn't denied that grossly negative market-share figures would negatively affect their lives.

As populations grow and society changes, it is difficult for the fearful to keep up, ironically because they often feel the need to deny that they're being left behind, but fear leads to denying the problem. The Internet age, with its rapid expansion of information, can exacerbate the problem. John McCain's campaign for the presidency may have been serious hurt in that he didn't use the Internet, not even email.

Modern finances carry new risks for confusion and fear. Should you write a check or use a debit card? What are the risks of using plastic credit regularly, and on the Internet? Is a home equity loan a good idea? Those are just starters. Denial of such issues can make you susceptible to fraud or direct theft, confined to using a limiting cash system, financial failure, and other limitations.

We also have more laws in these times. We have more neighbors, more guns, and at least more awareness of crime. Being able to consider unknown consequences has become more important as society develops. Not denying fear could remind us to lock our cars when we get out, and when we get in. In denial, many still even leave their keys in the car. We can't always stop something like being carjacked, or having our car stolen, but we can make it more difficult. Seat belts have been available a long time, but some drivers deny the thousands of times that seat belts save lives for fear of the few times they might trap us in a burning car. Even worse, sometimes seat belts are left unfastened just because they're uncomfortable.

RISK TAKING

Fearfulness of home invasions can lead to having a home security plan that might even include knowing how and when to use guns. Not denying this fear can thus lead to feeling reasonably secure, where fear of dangerous unknowns can easily become incapacitating. Although we do have to accept that we can't prepare for every possibility, recognizing these fears helps us appreciate that we're protecting being really alive, not entrapping ourselves in a cage of denial and undetermined fears.

When people are in denial about their fear of the unknown, they tend not to plan at all. Such denial can keep them from taking the kinds of risks that lead to growth. It can also lead to taking risks they shouldn't have taken. Even if we're stuck in a violent neighborhood, acknowledging our fears and considering them in our plans will help us choose where, or at least when, to go outside our homes. It might even help us find a way not to be stuck in our situation.

There are much less complicated examples to help us understand the role of denial in risk taking. Skydiving is often considered exciting fun, but it would be important to ask if the fun is worth the risk of things going wrong. Participating in rodeos, bull-fights, air shows, and many commonly accepted activities may involve excitement and possibly money, both of which might cloud the role of denial. Life has many dangers, but risking them may need more incentive than being simply for entertainment.

People usually start in high-risk activities at a young age. Many young people seem to have no fear of doing things like acrobatics on skate-boards over concrete. For them, the neurology of consequences isn't fully developed. Some get hooked on the excitement and continue into their older years. Sometimes the responsibilities of older people—concern for wives, children, mortgages, and so on—are then also denied.

Playing it safe doesn't mean that we don't take considered risks, especially when the risk is only emotional, not violent. Some people fear a promotion at work because they don't think they can do the job. That can be wise if we know more about ourselves than our employers have discovered. It can obviously be detrimental to our possibilities if we are in denial and just fearful about our abilities for some reason. Some people fear going out on any limb. It's true that limbs can be cut off, but such risks can be weighed. It's a balancing problem and denial can confuse the issues.

Denial is how we avoid clear thinking about things that we would otherwise be able to do. Buying an inexpensive car with credit when the old one is causing problems is usually a good risk if you really need a car. Buying a luxury car on credit doesn't make as much sense as the joy of prestige doesn't balance well with denying the possibility of financial pain or disaster. Leaping into marriage smacks of denial about divorce. Taking five years to decide that a marriage has a good chance of working is probably a denial issue as well. Our fears need to be taken seriously, considered thoroughly.

THINKING ISSUES THROUGH

When we're in denial, what we often don't do is a genuine investigation of what it takes to be successful. For example, what it takes to make a marriage work or to make a wise financial decision. Such thinking could generate a good deal of denial, or of wisdom, depending on how we handle our fear. We don't tend to think much about fear being a common factor in daily living. This is a good example of denial.

Some fear provides safety. Some is limiting to the fullness of our lives. Denial can result in a difficulty making wise choices. We can't always be correct in our choices, but investigating what frightens us about them is wise. That's the point where we most likely discover the blindness we've had in regard to denial.

Sometimes our fears are about known consequences. These can be fairly simple, like not having enough money for basic needs. They can be complex, like what is expected from a marital relationship. There are times when we can't find a solution, even to a known problem, but considering our fears is usually critical to the best solution if there is one. Losing ourselves in a marriage should be frightening. Thinking about the give-and-take, including standing up for ourselves, no matter how frightening, will help us find the positive rewards and avoid getting damaged.

ANXIETY

Psychologists study fear by measuring anxiety levels. Anxiety is an unpleasant experience, and it has a tendency to become worse before it gets better. It's important to know that specific anxiety always gets better. The body can only tolerate so much and lets it go even when that's not a good idea. Combat veterans who've been in a protracted firefight know the experience. Anxiety can be highly debilitating, and constantly returns if nothing else changes, so resolving its causes is important. Denying anxiety really can't be done without drugs, but it is fairly easy to deny the causes of it.

Doing something about sources of anxiety is the healthy response. That means you have to avoid denying what is frightening you. When we deny a frightening element, we are likely denying that we fear it's unfixable. Usually we're just afraid of hard decisions that need to be made. The unhealthy response, often prescribed by physicians, is to artificially avoid the anxiety through drugs, busyness, or other avoidance techniques. Anxiety avoided returns with a vengeance when the situation continues.

Those of us called *agoraphobic* illustrate the problem best. We didn't start our lives that way. The term loosely means afraid of so many things that we would rather stay at home than go out for any reason. The diagnosis usually is given to us in our twenties or later. Unfortunately, such people usually develop relationships—I wouldn't call them friends or professionals—who protect them from facing their fears, thinking they're being helpful. The list of limitations of such a response to fears is too long; let's just call it not really living.

I know the story of an eight-year-old who had enough support from his primary caregivers that he was able to face an extreme fear early in his life. Briefly left home alone in his large house with a full basement, he was frightened by a noise in the basement. The stairs to the basement were the kind that a monster could reach through and grab you by the ankles. To get to those stairs, a person would have to go through a locked door just to turn on a light. He had never risked doing that before, even with his parents at home.

He decided to sit near the front door and wait for his parents. He knew the neighbors, but those houses and his had shrubs and shadows around them. It didn't occur to him that the phone would be of help. His parents didn't come, and didn't come. He began to sweat and couldn't think any good thoughts. Finally, for him, it became easier to check the door than try to wait out the anxiety. The locked door was opened quietly. With the lights turned on, and a shout of *who's there,* he went down the stairs very quickly. He was still alive, and no monsters were found. He was no longer anxious.

It would be a whole other issue if a trauma had resulted from his bravery, but by facing these fears, he kept the possibilities of a full life open. At his young age, this child learned to think through his fears, weigh risks against shut-up-ness, and muster the courage to beat back urges for denial. This can be learned after being attacked by the real monsters of life; it's just harder and often needs support from those who understand.

EMOTIONS

All too often, fear of emotions in general was learned in childhood. Children are sometimes shunned or even punished for having emotions. Such families can be devoid of emotions, leading to children with little experience in understanding their own feelings. Then strong emotions are easily frightening. Occasionally, emotions are overly reinforced or not regulated, leading to harsh social effects. Sometimes rejection by someone more mature, or just the fear of being out of control or incapacitated, leads to denial. Once you get out in the world, there is little support for poor regulation of emotions.

We can't be out in the world very long without experiencing that some of our behaviors lead to rejection. It can be especially harsh when it isn't anticipated. Fearing rejection can close down a person. Denying such experiences can lead to a vague uneasiness. Dealing with rejection is inhibited by pain, fear that we deserved it, not knowing what else to do, and several other complicated issues. If people don't deny that the rejections happen, or that they can find solutions, then life can remain large, and such problems can be resolved temporarily or even permanently.

We need both security and defenses to handle our fear of rejection. The more security we feel, the less defensiveness we will need. Highly secure people are accepted enough that rejection mostly feels like a situation just wasn't the right fit. They rarely fear looking into why a relationship didn't work. Were they reaching beyond their skills in an employment application? Did they not realize an imbalance of power in their relationship that led to frightening their friend?

When we're in an intimate relationship, rejection is often an immature denial-response to fear. In denial, rejecting first when fearing rejection can feel better. Facing the issues opens the possibility of everything from our fears being a mistake to ending the situation without having to reject the other. Life can be more, but fear of a bigger life might itself be a part of the denial problem. Here is that issue of personal security again. When we're not secure enough, our defensiveness come up. Then anger easily feels like a solution and hides our denial of the problem.

There are many levels of fear. It's always valuable to notice if we're finding some thought intolerable, and if it's a life or death issue. Having fear for intolerable thoughts is greatly different than fear of a situation that is life-threatening. The latter fear can save our life; the former may be inhibiting our growth and our happiness.

Facing our denial is like so many life issues: We have to find a balance between too much and too little fear. A walk in the woods can be a beautiful experience if our fear of animals leads to precautions. Not in denial, we can notice what went wrong when hikers make the news. With too much fear, we're in danger of not enjoying a hike, or hiking without preparation due to denial.

RELATIONSHIPS

Finding a balance when we enter a new intimate relationship is far more complex than hiking in the woods. Many appear to deny that relationships can range from relatively easy to deadly. Further troubling, easy relationships can be a bigger problem than complex ones. There is often something deceptive about an easy relationship, and just feeling good about someone right away can also hide issues that need to be considered. To have some fear about a relationship is usually a healthy approach.

Psychologists have found that it's quite common to like or dislike a person in the first few minutes of meeting, but that's not an issue of just charm. We're drawn to relationships for a multitude of issues and not all of them are healthy. If we're not in denial, it's fairly easy to notice if a charming person is too out of balance. The best relationships usually start out without even the charm of dating—where only best behaviors are seen.

When two people have a reason to be together, talk together, and like what they experience, the chances that they've found a friend are good. With a start like that, fearing whether the relationship will work out may represent too much fear. Not noticing if the situation significantly changes represents too little fear. Time is a significant test regarding the quality of a relationship, but is rarely considered when we're in denial.

DEALING WITH FEAR

If we're healthy enough to fear behaviors with known negative consequences, we still need to know that what we do with our fear matters. As noted earlier, fear is known to build to a peak and then diminish. Avoided before this diminishment, it can return stronger than before. Avoided after it peaks, it can still return, but weakened. If we've learned this factor by experience, we are far less likely to use denial about known fears. Denial is easy if we haven't learned that fear diminishes on its own over time if you stay with it.

Imagine that a friend wants us to ski a black diamond run. Perhaps we hadn't thought we had the skill for such a run. We may feel fear, perhaps even recalling a skiing accident in the news. If we quickly say no, we allow our fear to be stronger if asked again. If we address the fear and recognize our ability to slow down if we feel we're getting out of control, our fear will diminish and our decision will be more likely based on the facts of our skill. Poor decisions based on relationship or ego will be far less likely, and our activity will be less dangerous.

How much denial we allow into decisions about fearful things determines our balance between happiness and sadness, safety and danger. Dealing with this aspect of denial is a learned set of skills. When a parent models facing fears, children find the skill easy to pick up. On our own, this may take more practice. Having friends with such abilities helps. Avoiding denial is usually not a uniform skill. We may find that we do well with some aspects of our life and poorly with others.

What we will learn, if we practice, is that denial of fears is not only unhelpful, it can be dangerous. The need for practice is a challenge of patience. The behavior isn't automatic; there will be failures. On every step of the road, fear can disrupt progress again. Rachmaninoff hated making mistakes while playing the piano, so he practiced a lot. He was quite successful even though he still made mistakes. If we don't like a known dangerous-though-important behavior, we have to practice with our knowledge of the dangerousness. Many, but not all, mistakes can be eliminated.

Denial is rampant with regard to fears, possibly because we tend to be embarrassed about being fearful. Perhaps the overly fearful have given fear a bad name. At a healthy level, fear can be quite useful. To make progress with denial related to fear, we have to start with acceptance. It's of little value just to know how healthy our level of fear is. In fact, it could trick us into either denial or complacency.

Knowing how we approach fear, and accepting that knowledge, is a skill everyone needs for maturation. Our history of experiences determines what we'll be fearful of and how fearful we'll be. Police officers need a controllable level of fear every time they approach a stopped car for any reason, or they can easily forget their safety training. Some of us couldn't be police officers. Many in law enforcement enjoy the excitement of fear, especially if it's not clearly intense.

The issue isn't about how much fear to allow in our lives; it's about how we face the fears we find there. Do we make decisions based on awareness or clouded by denial? Fear can't be completely avoided, but it can be denied. The results of such denial range from a diminished life to death. Acceptance of that which frightens us usually leads to a safer and fuller life, often even a happier one.

STEPS THAT MAY DEEPEN UNDERSTANDING:

1. List those things that cause fearfulness in you. Then rate them as to realistic level of risk.

2. Evaluate the role of your self-esteem. Do you generally feel capable of overcoming risks?

3. Learn about "touch and release." When realistic risk is low, don't ignore the risk, but think about it briefly and then move on to other ideas.

4. Use critical thinking. Ask yourself if you are just using the thoughts of others or thinking the issue through for yourself.

5. Work on emotional and rational regulation. Discuss your level of regulation of these issues with a friend, or at least write them down and clearly evaluate your experiences.

STEPS FOR DEALING WITH RECURRING FEAR

It usually happens at night, but anytime we feel overcome by fear, whether it's a quiet sense of dread or outright panic, the following steps are often found effective:

1. Acknowledge emotions.

2. Briefly accept past experiences that may be surfacing in the current feelings and thoughts. Fear is always based in experiences.

3. Acknowledge that the current fear is real and possible. Loved ones might already be dead. A physician could have missed how sick we really are. Our business enterprise really might not survive the current situation. The potential lawsuit, storm, earthquake, whatnot could happen. Do this briefly.

4. Question whether the fear is providing us anything to do about the circumstances bringing on the emotions. If a noise has startled us, we may need to check out what caused it, or even call the police for assistance.

5. If the middle-of-the-night situation checks out as safe, and we haven't found anything to validate

the fears, then we need to rationalize that sleep will be relaxing, refreshing, and good for overall health and happiness.

6. Now the work begins. Try to visualize or otherwise imagine a pleasant thought, place, sound, or scene. This will take some discipline until it's habit. If not successful in a minute or two, repeat the prior steps. Remember that sustaining fear emotions is not healthy, is not a solution, and is a habit containing denial of what we've reminded ourselves of in the initial steps.

7. If what we fear happened in the night, do not try to go to sleep, just contemplate how soon it will come using pleasant thoughts. If we struggle at this change, even that is better than fear, and will likely lead to sleep in a fair amount of time.

8. If the fear arises in the midst of daily activities, we can just substitute physical activities for the pleasant thoughts.

Nothing in life is to be feared.
It is only to be understood.

Marie Curie

Chapter Six
RULES

If we're to overcome the fear and other supporting factors of denial, we may need something artificial, something not natural to our current culture. That can be rules. Creating conscious rules often isn't what we naturally do and may feel artificial. Being consistently aware of our rules for living will feel different. Sometimes rules are needed when our habits, or unconscious rules—though natural feeling—aren't working. Once we accept that we have a problem, and that it's a strong, well-practiced habit, we will need to set some rules if effective and enduring change is our goal.

Most of us accept certain rules for healthy living. It may even amaze us how easily we "lose" or forget them. Our parents may have taught us some of them. Others, we may have had to learn. Any new rules we learn that don't become habits are often difficult to maintain. It takes the patience developed by understanding to practice healthy living long enough for it to become a habit.

Like living, many games can become chaotic if participants don't play by the rules. In football, the rules are well established and closely policed. The game wouldn't be much fun if team members could make up their own rules. Without rules, most games would be diminished by unfairness. Rules establish what's fair in games, and in life, and rules are important for overcoming denial.

It's disappointing when your favorite team has a touchdown called back due to a holding charge, but it's well understood that the score would often be different if the rule hadn't been broken. Unfortunately, the rules of life aren't always as clear, as well policed, or even always as fair. Many of life's rules are personal and individualistic. Even when we believe that flossing our teeth is beneficial, the belief has to be made into a rule, and then self-enforced. When consequences may be well down the road, we need to believe in the rule as well as the consequences.

Modern societies establish rules about living together; when taken to legislatures, they are laws. Some are long lasting, and generally accepted. Society's rules are meant to protect the public, but are subject to bias, and can succumb to politics. Such rules are sometimes challenged out of a desire the rules inhibit. Some have been challenged, such as those based on racism and sexism, as society matures. When the issues are complex, rules easily lose their power to correct behaviors. They become more subject to denial.

Many laws, even traffic laws, are less policed than those for organized games. Strictly obeying them has to do with our attitude. We usually can break speed laws, for instance, if we don't waiver too far from the rule. We may be aware that we might face a fine, but we're often in denial about the dangers of driving fast. Laws are so black and white that they rarely fit all situations. This can lead to a situation that is fertile ground for denying our responsibility for consequences.

OUR PERSONAL RULES

We have a further risk of denial in our personal lives: our rules aren't lived in front of an umpire. As adults, we often act as the authority and the observer. We might think that following our own rules would be easier. That might be true of rules we've clearly considered with regard to their value and consequences, and that we've practiced over time. However, many of our rules have been handed down and are not clearly understood or completely accepted.

We may have been told to eat vegetables without clearly understanding the value of the rule. Our parents may not have consistently explained the reason for or enforced the rule either. In the day to day, the rule may not have seemed to matter. Denial can hide any consequences until we're old and desire better health. An observer can ascertain rules in our lives, but we often don't feel we're specifically living by many.

The rules that especially fool us are the ones about breaking our rules. These easily become an elixir for denial if we don't notice that we're hedging our own rules. Sometimes delay easily becomes a new habit, which can especially become important when we need to use rules to change habits. The first step is the use of a rule for raising consciousness, the opposite of denial. If we discover the danger of speeding, we can more easily enforce our own rule not to speed. Psychology calls this internalizing the rule. We can become our own policeman for our rules.

When we deny our need for rules, we deny that we need to change or regulate something. We can become stuck, or headed on the road to despair. Maintaining status quo is the shut-up-ness that Kierkegaard warned can lead to despair. No matter how good we feel about ourselves, personal change is the way to maintain good feelings. Denial of a need to follow new rules is the opposite of acceptance. Learning to formulate rules that we can follow makes accepting encountered difficulties easier.

Life is dynamic. Change is necessary, often over fairly short lengths of time. Status quo usually doesn't really exist. It is a figment of denial. When we maintain anything that needs changing, things often become worse. For example, when couples don't resolve small issues that irritate, hidden angers become expressed and attitudes harden. Then the relationship can die from social rigor mortis. Establishing rules about trying to resolve such issues is the right medicine.

Rules have to be examined and made personal to avoid denial and to consistently affect a person's behaviors. Once personal, rules must be supported by a clear awareness of the consequences of breaking the rule. Unexamined rules are rarely very effective in an individual's life. When rules aren't effective, the consequences can be anything from disastrous to mildly frustrating. Denial can easily take over when the consequences are small, and can be seen in the repeat of disastrous situations as well.

Although they may argue about what is too much, few people don't believe in a rule to not eat too much. Many of us break this rule when food is tasty, unless we learned as a child to stop eating when we were full. Yes, we get uncomfortable for a while when breaking this rule. The problem is exacerbated by potions that quickly relieve such discomfort, such as antacids. The terrible down-the-road consequences of obesity are rarely considered.

EARLY LEARNING ABOUT RULES

As children, we likely were confused about rules when our parents punished us for breaking them. Punishment may have led to feeling badly about ourselves right when we needed to feel smart about things we were learning. Much of what we learn about rules as children comes from finding that we broke them, or that they were more important to our parents than we thought. Too often, we basically learn to look out for our parents more than to look out for consequences. Even pre-school children do better with rules if they've been explained and the consequences discussed.

Let's consider the rule about a place for everything and everything in its place that people with certain compulsions think is a fine rule. Such people believe that following this rule is less frustrating than putting things down any place when through with them. These people find comfort in knowing where to find things. Those of us who aren't remarkably compulsive find it easier to leave things out or put them away in the most convenient locations.

It's a matter of having different rules: find quickly or be done with it quickly. Such personal rules are usually well practiced, and difficult to change. Both approaches work until they become a waste of time and energy. Over time, the way in which these rules don't work can become self-esteem issues. Each of these rules can breed worries, especially when in conflict with others. Unattended worries of error don't facilitate good self-esteem.

Denial can enter here: We can develop excuses or even defenses for our behaviors, which is denial. Compulsive people may benefit by being aware of whether their behavior rule is mostly to gain emotional comfort or an efficiency issue. Those less compulsive can often benefit by becoming aware if they are running themselves down when they can't find something they used last.

One person may argue that the rule just makes sense, and the other, that they do eventually find everything. Avoidance of solutions to either issue is denial. Often, such avoidance has to do with feeling helplessly out of control, and this is where using rules can help with change. Following any rule successfully requires self-control, even if the rule is to avoid trying to control everything, especially other people, or to avoid being controlled.

FURTHER LEARNING ABOUT RULES

Rules are helpful if they help us avoid feeling out of control, but we often have a negative reaction to rules. Rules probably get a bad reputation in elementary school, where they are all too often something to memorize rather than something to understand. Often teachers aren't left with enough time to discuss with pupils why one way is better than another in certain situations. Then students just receive a red check mark or circle, are told they're wrong, and have to follow some rule. Rules can then feel arbitrary, which also makes them difficult to remember.

Like some children, adults know we don't have to follow all rules, but we're usually more aware than children of the consequences if we don't follow most of them. Consider speed limits again. Some of us disagree that the faster we drive, the more likely we could be in a terrible accident. Some argue about keeping up with traffic, but such arguments don't cancel out the data on speed, reaction times, and accidents. Neither does being an excellent driver with a good record. Such arguments can be seen as denial.

Speed limits don't always make sense, but following them does. Sometimes, if we make our own rules, we enforce denial. Yes, there are places that the speed limit seems too slow, but do we know about the children who live in those homes? Speed limits are a legislative guess as to what would be the safest. We're also in denial if we think we can always safely travel at the posted limit. Sometimes conditions don't allow for travel at such speeds. Denial easily allows us to break traffic rules if the authorities aren't around. It's like a doctor telling us to go on a thousand-calorie diet. When we're in denial, we say that the doctor doesn't understand and he's not watching. In such a case, the doctor may give up and not mention it again.

We have to be careful not to let a lack of authorities mislead us into not feeling responsible for our behavioral choices. An absent police officer doesn't mean that it's safe to speed. An absent doctor isn't permission to slowly die from the ugly complications of obesity. No one understands us as well as we can, which often makes advice ineffectual. Letting others be responsible for us is a trick of denial. It can give us someone else to blame for our failures in lieu of taking responsibility for ourselves. Our parents were responsible for us at least until our teenage years, but they needed to gradually teach us to take over this crucial self-responsibility.

Even when we wisely choose our own rules, denial is awaiting in our discouragement. Whether we break our own rules with conscious intent or by a slip or several slips, we need to support our use of them until we see progress. Then the task of supporting our new rules becomes much easier. Whether were trying to change an eating or driving pattern we can see the benefits of a new rule if we review it and stick to it.

Perhaps we realize that a rule prevented an accident. For example, by driving slowly we stopped just short of a car that pulled in front of us from a driveway. Or perhaps, we realize that we lost a few pounds after establishing a rule to avoid having cheese and crackers with a beer every afternoon. Reviewing such events is important to keep our rule in our active consciousness.

MAINTAINING OUR RULES

When we make new rules, we need to note their potential and how much struggle we may experience to follow them. The more often new rules work, the easier it is to get through that initial period of frequent failure to follow our own advice. After each breach, we can notice the probable consequences over time. One lapse by itself doesn't lead to failure unless we say to ourselves that the lapse doesn't matter.

If our self-esteem is badly damaged, the lapse can be interpreted as mattering too much. We may think we're never going to get better, or even that we might as well not try. Establishing rules about thoughts like that can help us develop our self-esteem. We may need a person, or people, around us who believe in the positive process until we get the hang of it.

Blaming ourselves, our parents, or our society doesn't help. It does help to know that we didn't develop the problem in a vacuum. It's even more important to know if our problem has a neurological component. The part of our brain that checks on consequences before a behavior, that limits impulsivity, isn't known to be fully developed before the age of 25. It might be wise to hold back driving permits and drinking privileges until that age. I doubt that would happen, but let me make the point: The development of these parts of the brain is influenced by parenting experiences, especially in the first year of life, and social experiences.

We are learning more and more about how such experiences affect neurological development and even gene expression in developing children. The more developmental problems we have, the more we need rules. Criminologists have found that young men with multiple felonies sometimes have about half of the brain cells needed for impulse control that other young men have.

The problem is furthered in that we don't just attempt to control criminal behavior, we punish the criminal. Such an approach is an example of denial, as punishment can even reinforce a behavior, and it certainly doesn't help a criminal feel like a good person.

When we feel like a good person we find it easier to develop internal rules that support good behavior.

Our attitude about criminals is a vicious circle. Parents who don't have the time or the knowledge to train a child well end up making their children feel that they aren't any or very good. School personnel also often don't have the time and training to correct problems, and even all too frequently make problems worse. Then the criminal justice system steps in and treats criminals like the scum of the earth.

Society as a whole is far from ready to feel safe treating criminals as though their primary problem is neurological. Thus, treatment rarely focuses on rationally learning rules for behaviors that aren't naturally supported by neurological development. I think the future will show that learning rules related to criminal behavior isn't that different from learning rules for healthy eating.

It will be very difficult to have the public understand that punishing criminals makes social problems worse. People in most developed countries don't understand this issue in regard to punishing their own children, let alone criminals. The fear of being called irresponsible supports denial of this issue. The trouble is that such denial holds back both parents and society.

To mature, we need to be held responsible for our behaviors, but not have our character judged. Blaming a person for mistakes implies we clearly know what we're doing. Such thinking appears more naïve as we understand further about neurological development.

I'm not saying that people don't need to be locked up for dangerous behaviors. Even recidivist drug users need to be locked up. However, they don't need to be treated badly if we want treatments to work.

In essence, rules are developed in effective treatments. If a person with criminal thinking and behaviors is to be helped, it has to start by treating them with respect. Then mutual respect is far more possible and strategies can be shared. When the understanding isn't there to respect society's rules, the thoughts about consequences need to be developed. When such people even suspect a behavior might cause them harm, they can then consider what socially successful people would do in their situation.

That's a perfect use of new rules to overcome neurological deficits, and staying out of trouble with the law would reinforce them. Rules can help people overcome a neurological deficit that makes impulsive behavior far too unrestricted. The task isn't easy, but it's facilitated when a problem has been acknowledged and people feel good about themselves, even if they don't feel good about some of their behaviors.

If our brain has built-in behavioral deficits, we must develop new rules as a preventative measure. Criminals need to recognize that they just aren't quick enough in noticing consequences to their behaviors. The consequences are often more dramatic, but similar to driving too fast and eating too much. They need to develop and practice rules that keep them from being hurt or hurting others.

FROM RULES TO HABITS

At first, we consciously and rationally develop rules to adjust to neurological deficits. In effect, we say to ourselves this is how I would like to behave. With patient practice, we develop such rules with physical support within the brain. New neurological connections support a new habit. Then rules require less and less conscious support.

Life is much easier when the rule just occurs to us in time to inhibit a behavior. For example, when I was young, as soon as I saw black-and-white car, my foot came off the gas. Then law enforcement started using radar and it took four tickets in one year for me to develop new rules about the speed I chose to drive. Within a few years, without even consciously thinking about it, my foot came off the gas whenever I saw my speed above the limit. I've had one speeding ticket since that time, and it was the result of buying oversized tires without knowing it. I thought I was traveling a safe few miles over the limit when I was actually ten miles over.

Some of this physical change in the brain is from practice of new neural pathways and neglect of the old ones, and some of it's the expression of genes. I don't pretend to understand genetic development very well, but it has become clear to me that social developments express genes that were potential before they we set into action. No matter what our age, we are not stuck with our old programs; change just takes practicing our rules.

EXCUSES AND JUSTIFICATIONS

Two of the main ways we express denial are by using excuses and justifications. They are mostly used to avoid frustration and despair. We usually put them in play when a challenge causes us to wonder if something is wrong with us. We've lost a friend, or even a job, and the cause is clear: We were covering our insecurity by dominating conversations, and not listening to others, or something like that.

Without new rules, we easily retreat to excuses and justifications; we use denial of our responsibility for our problems. We're sometimes trying to deny that we even have problems. Our denial is usually based in the fear that we can't change. We've probably failed at trying to change ourselves and didn't realize that we just didn't know how. We've probably even denied our fear. Such denial is rarely completely successful and leaves us with a lingering doubt about our well-being.

Those of us who have successfully avoided this problem don't wonder such things; we know there are things wrong with us. For us, it isn't as frightening. Sometimes finding a problem is almost contemporaneous with fixing it. We've learned to believe in our ability to change if we see the need. However, it's usually not that easy. Serious problems are well entrenched, well protected. Care must be taken that we don't just get used to our problems, as that is a way to deny their consequences.

If our limitations don't appear to have serious consequences, the issue may have to do with a limitation of acceptance. We may be accepting who we are without accepting who we can be. We've denied consequences with excuses and justifications. Chapter Four discussed the issue of healthy and unhealthy acceptance further.

Accepting that we're stuck in a life far short of what we once envisioned is unhealthy acceptance. Some goals may need revision, but accepting our mistakes is essential for progress. Only then do limitations become changeable. In healthy acceptance, we know that there is no end to finding corrections for our lives, and that we can continually make progress with them. We learn to use rules.

Rules only feel artificial until we form new habits. We design them with our rational self. Because they're artificial, they take time before we remember to use them regularly. Motivation can also be a problem until we experience the positive effect of a new rule. Further, the new rule may not be an effective one. If so, it will need to be thrown away or modified, but we must be careful that some denial factor hasn't impeded the rule's effectiveness.

PATIENCE AND ACCEPTANCE

Impatience may be a factor debilitating a good rule's effectiveness. Not noticing such a factor can be another form of denial. Accepting that we are impatient, for example, is recognition of the honesty we need to make successful changes. Once we've accepted a dynamic limitation, and we want to change it, we can find support by noticing negative consequences of a similar limitation in someone else's life.

Now that I've made a rule to avoid talking more than my share in social situations, I have realized that many people talk more than their share, and suffer negative consequences. I'm aware, that, like I was, they probably have no idea that they talk far more than others in groups, or that it's not appreciated. There can be many reasons for this phenomenon. I found both social insecurity and arrogance at the core of my problem, but the insight didn't lead to any progress. My wife shared her embarrassment, which helped me focus, but I had to see the negative consequences and form some rules to change.

Thus, I accepted that I had a problem. Denying it would likely have led to thinking that social talk was boring without my brilliant input. I was close to that, if not fully guilty of it. Denying it would have regarded my wife's input as wrong, and might even have damaged our relationship. In the past when I occasionally ran into someone with the same problem as mine, I'm sure we didn't like each other as we contested for verbal space.

I was also denying that I didn't have balanced friendships. Getting a discussion going with my acquaintances was difficult. I now feel certain that it wasn't much fun discussing anything with someone who was so sure of himself, and so full of talk. It amazes me how effective acceptance was after establishing one simple rule: don't talk as much as any of the top half of any group of talkers.

What I found was that, whenever I remembered my rule, I was one of the quiet ones. When I added a rule for not quickly talking back to a person, I wasn't talking much at all. My wife had long complained that I frequently interrupted her when she was speaking. I finally figured out that my quick responding was interrupting her thoughts. In denial, I just thought I was a great listener: Sensitive and intuitively knowing what she was saying, and was going to say. What I was missing was that she felt interrupted and didn't like it.

I once went to a meeting with eight psychologists. I was remembering my rule pretty well by then. I literally counted how many of us were around a conference table and divided that into the number of minutes the meeting was expected to take. With a rule that limited myself through these mathematics, I learned more from the discussion that day than I usually experienced in such meetings. More relevant to me, I think I am more liked and respected now than when I was basically showing off in a disrelational way.

DEVELOPING EFFECTIVE RULES

It is amazing how following a well thought-out rule can dramatically change an entrenched behavior. First, of course, we have to get out of denying the behavior. I can't begin to fully describe such denial: It can reach as deep as feeling so empty and vulnerable that any helpful comment feels like an attack, as opposed to a legitimate criticism. Then rules will be needed for that issue. Effective rules would consider the source of the confrontation: Is this an enemy or friend, for example.

Appreciating the courage that a friend needs to confront us might be helpful. We may be denying that we have an important problem behavior. We might be viewing our friend as rude, picky, impolite, or something other than helpful. Checking their demeanor is helpful. A rule to take a breath and slow the conversation down is also quite helpful.

When people obviously have many thick layers of denial, we experience them as defensive. We may respect them, even enjoy listening to them, but we will know that we're not in relationship with them. We're likely to also quickly experience that disagreeing, perhaps even adding a thought, usually doesn't add to the relationship. Well-educated professional people especially need to investigate the issue. Many psychologists and physicians, for example, would likely both be more effective and easier to relate to if they looked into such problems, and developed some rules.

This task of making rules can start in many places. If we think we don't have problems, and haven't been fortunate enough to have a respected person challenge us about such issues, then we have to start by noticing that our life isn't perfect. If we think we're close enough to perfect, we need to beware of denial about the importance of personal progress, which can be hidden by financial and professional success. It may be helpful to inquire of ourselves whether we're happy after a workday, and whether we anticipate being happy if we can't work any longer.

Wherever we start, accepting that we will be happier with personal progress, and accepting that we see difficulty we've ignored, is the first step. If fear or some defensiveness then holds us back from acceptance, we need to take another step back. This could mean remembering the pressure to get all "A"s in school, and feeling like perfection was the expectation. Acceptance is certainly much easier when perfection isn't an issue.

When we've accepted an issue that is holding us back from more happiness, then forming rules is the next step. The first rule is often just to accept a problem that we've discovered. Then we need some research to find a rule that works. Often our first rule at such a point is too complex or otherwise too demanding. Such rules quickly slip out of our consciousness. Weeks later, we may notice an old issue and be surprised that we haven't been following our rule.

Sometimes such a rule needs to be simplified. The rule may be fine, but a rule may be needed to remember the rule. For example, if you've created a rule about not bringing work home so you can have more family time, a note on your briefcase could be as simple as "THINK." Such supporting rules on simple notes can be posted in places that remind us of the issues at hand: On a mirror, a briefcase, the refrigerator, the rear-view mirror, the TV, or any place that's related to an accepted problem.

Once we've decided to gently seek personal change, the way we choose an issue to address is often important. It's common, and perhaps a trick of denial, to choose a deeply entrenched issue that will discourage us if we don't already have a history of success with personal change. Finding an easier issue to address initially may embarrass those of us who think of ourselves as quite successful. If an initial rule is too difficult, it will be important to remember that we can create another rule if the rule chosen begins to discourage us from making any changes.

One last caution: success is less likely the more rules we work on at a time. Even focusing on one rule can require a rule or two in support of it. We often, for example, need a rule to keep trying or to modify our rule when necessary. Patience truly is a virtue when it comes to our maturation. Perfection in humans is always a bluff. Progress comes from skill. Denial is the devil in the details. Working on a skill is often best done with a mentor, or at least a companion in the task, but it can certainly be done alone.

STEPS THAT MAY DEEPEN UNDERSTANDING:

1. If you've resisted rules, reflect on how you developed that attitude.

2. Make all rules your own: that is, make sure they are really what you want for yourself.

3. Discard rules that are no longer needed, or just don't make sense. For example, you may have needed a specific rule to eat a certain amount of vegetables and now find that you just enjoy them enough that a rule isn't needed.

4. Be sure to have a gentle rule about breaking your rules. "No labelling, just patience," is a good example.

5. Evaluate the conditions when you have broken rules. Ask if the rule was well chosen, won't break your patience before you've tasted success, and issues like that.

TIPS FOR CREATING SUCCESSFUL RULES

1. See if you feel the importance of personal change no matter how successful you feel you've been.

2. Question how you would feel if you experienced a significant change in family or employment.

3. Consider any training you experienced regarding being perfect. We often deny that we feel pressure to be perfect, or even that perfection isn't the human condition.

4. Take care in developing a first rule for a discovered issue. It's easy to make such rules far too complex and all encompassing.

5. Consider starting with a less important attitude or behavior than the one that you've focused on as a significant need for change.

*I don't like work—no man does—but I like what
is in work—the chance to find yourself.*

Joseph Conrad

CHAPTER SEVEN
EMPATHY

We need to be gentle with ourselves if we're to be successful noticing and avoiding a negative use of denial in our lives. Failures are to be expected whenever we take on any new and difficult task. When the task has to do with our personality, the complexity is great and our emotions are strongly involved. We will need a high level of empathy for ourselves, not just for others.

We usually think of empathy as our capacity to understand what others are going through. It's also a grand skill for understanding what we're going through. Too often we don't understand the complexities we face and defeat ourselves with negativity. This negativity is usually done with labels and is the opposite of empathy.

Empathy is a dynamic skill, one that needs to be continually developed. Even when our parents taught this skill by modeling a loving attitude, and we had behaviors guided by developmental understanding, the complexities of adult life will still require us to work more on our empathic skill. Issues like bias, prejudice, and simple ignorance, all challenge our ability to be empathetic.

Because empathy is about understanding, anything that blocks the truth of an issue limits empathy. Bias, for example, is rarely taken seriously enough and severely blocks us from deeply understanding a truth. Many of our strongly defended beliefs are a result of bias blinding us to critical thinking as to how our self-interest may have confused us.

Empathy has been described as walking in another's shoes, while fully aware you aren't the person. Not being aware of differences between you and another person may contaminate your empathy. When we exercise denial about ourselves, our empathy is usually also severely limited. It's a vicious cycle, as empathy often evades us when we don't fully understand ourselves.

When we're in denial, we aren't even walking in our own shoes. Accepting the possibility of denial in our lives, we find it easier to have empathy for ourselves and others. Many of us who are raised in a dominant culture are not well informed of these many differences between ourselves and persons of a different culture. The more we understand ourself, the more we become capable of empathy, including that for others. And, becoming increasingly empathetic is a critical element if we're to win our struggles with denial.

Empathy needs to be seen as a tool for progress. It helps us face our fears, develop our rules, and handle our failures well. Further, when we have empathy for ourselves, it facilitates patience for others through understanding. When we notice the role of empathy in our success, both personally and socially, our skill is reinforced and develops even more.

It's easy to notice any lack of empathy on our part when we catch ourselves being judgmental. We're probably judgmental when we not only pick what we think is right about some issue, but also condemn those with whom we disagree. Such arrogance can remind us of the work we have to do if we're to accept our immaturities and develop our personal security. Secure people less frequently deny the possibility of their own incorrectness, and are thus less judgmental of opinions that differ from theirs.

When we accept our own mistakes and win the struggle to overcome them, we become open to our incorrectness and to change, and then mistakes seem less frightening. It's far more difficult to accept mistakes if we think we'll be stuck with them. Understanding this struggle for personal growth is having empathy for ourself, and easily leads to empathy for others. We can thus use empathy as a measure of our growth in our own battle with denial.

The skill of being empathetic is both inherent in toddlers and learned. It's appears to be genetic and a natural result of effective parenting, but it needs to be developed. The good news is that it can be learned as an adult. The skill is central to the maturity that provides happiness. We may easily notice that we're in denial about our empathy skills (or lack thereof) if we're willing to do so. When we learn to recognize how a lack of empathy can cause us and others pain or failure in social situations, then our clarity can provide motivation for change.

THE ROLE OF PARENTS

With effective parenting, children develop empathy more naturally. Successful parents help infants develop a work ethic that is the basis for developing empathy. Love needs to be a given, but all else is best achieved by working for it. When children, even infants, learn to work to gain their desires, they are more likely to understand the struggles and failures of others as they grow up. If the learning environment is understanding and gentle, empathy is likely to develop.

At first, the learning is rudimentary and mostly unconscious. A simple cry earns the reward of a fresh diaper, food, and comfort. Before infants reach the age of two, many need to work at issues like holding back urges to bite and other impulsive behaviors. Biting can cause quite a stir and is kind of fun. When it is stopped, though otherwise ignored, empathy for one's self leads to not wanting to limit affection with the behavior. Punishing a child at that point, or even making a gentle fuss over the biting, gives the child attention, which then reinforces the behavior. In ignoring the behavior, once stopped, the rudiments of not harming others are developed.

The work ethic is learned time and again. At early stages, sharing is work and needs clear rewards to be learned. Dealing with the sharing issue, children can learn that empathy for themselves needs to be balanced with empathy for others. In fact, they are the same in many ways. By the time a child is a teenager, it should be clear to her that there is a correlation between sharing family work and using the family car.

I heard about a four-year-old (playing in a childcare center at a gym with his two-year-old brother) who understood the sharing issue. The staff was excited to tell his parents that, when another child stole a toy from the younger brother, the four-year-old quietly informed the "stealer" that his brother didn't know how to share yet, and took the toy back. When children understand that mistakes are just an issue of childhood development—not due to them being evil or stupid—they've learned a good deal about empathy, and develop social skills.

As children develop in a successful family, they aren't blamed for grabbing the last cookie on a plate; they're educated about the broader and more lasting rewards of sharing. By the time children are four years old, they begin to understand the process of childhood and develop empathy for themselves as learners, which easily develops into empathy for others.

Families have increasingly difficult responsibilities: They need more than simple affection and parental love. They need to understand child development. When parents deny their lack of this parenting skill, they tend to make demands of their children beyond a child's ability to understand. This leads to punishment for the child's "mistakes."

Children don't learn empathy very often in such environments. Usually, the lessons are fear, lying, and aggression. Lying and aggression usually have short-term rewards, and confuses the lesson of empathy. Psychologists have found a further complication in that punishment generally reinforces negative behaviors. Negative behaviors aren't positive social skills, and the outcome over time is always poor.

PERSONAL SECURITY

Empathy for others especially requires adequate self-esteem and personal security. These requirements are rarely developed in fear. It's easy to judge others when we don't understand how we all develop. The weapons of our judgmental attitude are negative labels, and labels can come back to haunt us. The lack of empathy works both ways: When we don't understand the struggles of others, we're unlikely to understand our own. When we call others stupid for not knowing something already, the label becomes easy to use on ourselves as surely we, too, don't know everything.

When we're in denial about devastation that could happen to us, we may have sympathy for those less fortunate than us, but we're unlikely to have empathy unless we feel our own vulnerability. Accepting awareness of how things could go badly for us makes us more cautious and resilient as long as we don't exaggerate our risks. Exaggerated risks tend to develop inactivity where little is learned. Risks are easily exaggerated when we dwell on an event like nuclear holocaust over which we have little control.

As we mature, we can develop a general empathy, giving everyone the right to make mistakes and not know everything. We may not know why someone lacks a social skill, but we generally understand that it's due to a lack of training, by themselves or others, not some moral or other inadequacy. Empathy allows us to inquire about our own lack of education, not lack of character, when we make a mistake. There's no end to life's complexities. It's one of the great values of life. Knowing that we can always learn more is the opposite of feeling stuck and bored.

DEVELOPING EMPATHY

We continue to develop our empathy throughout adulthood. Developing empathy is essential to beating denial, for empathy makes denial unnecessary. I was just slightly embarrassed when I realized that I had denied my social insecurity, and was dominating, even showing off, in groups of friends and others. I learned even more when noticing that I bragged about how I wasn't afraid to face the problem, and had made effective changes in myself.

Now, when I see someone dominating a conversation, I don't get bristly, I have empathy. My changes are then actually reinforced, and the old habit weakened. If I didn't experience empathy for someone who had yet to learn of something I'd learned, empathy for myself would work as a tool to remind me that I had more work to do on my denial. I would be likely to find that I lacked acceptance for some ego-protecting issue.

As previously noted, we can develop empathy as a child. That's the easiest way to start, but developing its quality in adulthood is crucial for happiness. Empathy can always be developed with awareness. And empathy can always become more sophisticated. That's good news for those who discover its value later in life. When we know the work we've done to change a behavior or an attitude, we're empathetic about a person still naïve or caught up in such a struggle. We don't try to change them, confront them or otherwise judge more than their behaviors. We may choose to leave dominated conversations, but we can do so without anger and revenge.

EMPATHY FOR BALANCE

Balancing the love of ourselves with the love of others is a tricky skill. Without empathy, the balance can slip either way. Love is usually found to be corrupted when it's out of balance. Denial easily shrouds issues like sex, neediness, and power. If we have developed a high quality of empathy for ourselves, then we don't tend to give ourselves away in love; we tend to notice whether or not what we get back is an adequate balance.

Empathy for ourselves is never about things or arrogance; it's about feeling worthwhile due to what we've earned with personal work. It's not about perfection; it's about being an effective human. Thus, a balance between loving ourselves and loving others is guided and supported by empathy. In a relationship, one person may have more to give at any one time than the other. The balanced isn't like a measure of weights; it's a measure of what one has to give and the other's ability to receive at the time.

In these give-and-take relationships, empathy can correct many pressures that can be overlooked in denial. When our needs for others are out of balance, denial is likely hiding these needs and offering other explanations. Sometimes the "explanations" are just attacks: "If you had dinner ready on time, I wouldn't be so angry." "I wasn't flirting, you're just jealous." Examples could go on and on.

Such justifications usually are examples of denial of using others, which is never successful over time. When we have empathy for the needs of others, and for ourselves in the long run, we avoid using others. By noticing a lack of empathy, if that's the case, we're prompted to accept whatever we are feeling insecure about, and get to work on dealing with how we've denied the problem. Domestic violence is the harshest example of denying using others. This violence confuses people unless they understand that abusers use the abused for their sense of well-being, and violence usually results from an extreme threat: the loss of the relationship.

If we are searching for respect, in contrast to gaining it through work, noticing our lack of respect for others can be quite effective. Then we may find we don't respect ourselves, and think that getting respect from others will fix the problem. We may even become aware that what we may have gained from our searches has been a false respect for ourselves. That can be the beginning of developing more empathy, and some genuine respect.

The rationale of searching for respect from others is rarely conscious, but fairly easy to accept once we confront a problem and learn to work on ourselves. The problem can be more complicated, like when we know we have respect, but it feels like it's never enough. The solution is the same: Notice the clues. Accept the problem. Work on it. That's the empathy solution.

EMPATHY CHALLENGES

People have many pressures in employment situations that often require a lack of respect for others. The first concern of a business is for their bottom line. Respect for their customers is also an issue, but secondary to profits. It's wise to make a decision to limit one's empathy for customers by business needs, but the practice needs to be artificial. We need concern that the practice is effective for us, and not damaging to our self-image. Salesmen are the easiest examples.

They rarely would have anyone's interests besides their own in making a sale. Their future in sales would be limited if they considered whether a client really needs what they're selling.

With adequate development of empathy, we are able to weigh situations. Are we denying that the stress of such work is hard on us? We must take care that we don't diminish our empathy for others in such a situation. As a teenager, I sold shoes in a high-pressure shoe store during the summer. I was often the top salesperson, and had the most return customers asking for me. I shared store policy with my customers: That I had to also show a similar shoe, a third product, and that I had to serve five customers at a time. I genuinely understood their frustration. Empathy helped me balance honesty with necessity. I think they felt my respect for them and respected my honesty about store policy. Sales people without empathy appeared to lose sales due to the intensity of their pressure.

We frequently discover that we have levels of honesty that need to be balanced with empathy. We like to think of honesty as pure and simple, but even honesty is limited, which then severely limits our empathy. We can only be honest about what we know, and the complexity of humans is a significant limitation. An easy illustration is being honest about loving another. When we don't have significant information about why we feel such love, we can't be sure of our level of honesty in this regard.

Honesty is about the truth, the whole truth, and nothing but the truth, but it can be diminished and even withheld out of empathy. For example, the "white lie" is usually deemed acceptable in many social contexts. The level and importance of a relationship determines how close to perfection our honesty needs to be. A person trusting their life and happiness in a relationship needs clear honesty. An acquaintance doesn't expect, and may even be taken aback by unmitigated honesty.

The truth can hurt both the receiver and the messenger. That needn't limit its use in mature relationships, where pain is likely to support growth. Telling a loved one that no, you don't prefer her new hair-style may be difficult, but will develop trust that is needed in other situations. However, empathy can sometimes be a legitimate limitation for telling the truth, even in mature relationships.

In a trusting love relationship, we often even share thoughts about behaviors. A prime example would be a thought about being sexually attracted to another. With empathy, just sharing such a thought, though painful, is adequate protection from the thought becoming behavior. Such sharing provides us with feedback beyond the skills of our own brain. However, sometimes we censor a thought as we feel we needn't risk bothering another. For example, if we've matured in our relationship with a loved one, why mention that a food-server is attractive?

Whether we really know a truth is itself a limitation on truth telling, and empathy leads to caution in this regard as well. The undoing of information we hold to be true can be a less harsh experience with appropriate empathy. This is a real issue in this age in which information is turned on its head on a regular basis. It isn't just being sure that the sun goes around the earth any more.

It is doubtful that anyone is honest all of the time. We all generally fall on a continuum of honesty, from being mostly honest except when we aren't to being mostly dishonest. Those who are dishonest most of the time are often addicted to a substance or a relationship. Regular lying feels required if one is to protect denial of behaviors of which we're usually not proud.

EMPATHY CORRUPTED BY DENIAL

Empathy is regularly corrupted by denial. It isn't that difficult to notice that we are hardly in an empathetic relationship when we're lying to others. However, it can at times feel like empathy. Such empathy is narrowly focused, namely, concern for artificially feeling good. It's a highly limited empathy, only good in the short term. It requires an urgent use of denial. To continue living with such a limited empathy, we must avoid its lack of effectiveness over time, and hide the harm to others from our consciousness.

At this low end of the honesty continuum, we can feel stress from the complexities of lying, which forms a vicious cycle. A poor decision made about feeling happy regardless of the consequences, made without awareness, usually requires more avoidance. In this miserable state, self-esteem suffers dramatically. Even if we recognize some empathy for our situation, without self-esteem, we would likely need empathy from another: a person who isn't judgmental and believes in our ability to change.

The lower our self-esteem, the more difficulty we may have in seeking help. Self-acceptance and hope that life can be more than the vicious downward spiral we've gotten ourselves into become crucial. When we've taken too many steps that feel like self-protection, only to find ourselves isolated from friends and other realities, believing in change becomes a dramatic leap of faith in humanity.

MAKING DECISIONS

At the higher end of this honesty continuum, people experience empathy knowing that the truth often hurts. In a mature relationship—with ourselves and others—being clearly honest is often most effective. Empathy helps us welcome honesty. Then experience supports the decision. We still need to consider whether we're ready to accept a particular truth as our friend. If we're unsure in such a decision, we can succumb to denial.

When we trust our empathy, we can consider potential consequences, and our ability levels, and usually make effective decisions. A person thinking about having a divorce is often in this situation. The consequences may be financial, the loss of friends, trouble for children, and many less-than-pleasant experiences for them and others. Their abilities would have likely already been tested, but seeking advice from friends and professionals may be needed at such an end-point.

When our empathy includes a long-range perspective on human development, we can balance all kinds of demands, not just levels of honesty. Most of our life is about meeting demands. With progress on accepting things that aren't effective, and focusing on our issues of denial, demands become less of a burden. Using empathy for balance, meeting the demands of life can be challenging, but we can enjoy the work.

Making choices about doing the work of life is agency, and lessens the demand aspects of our need for change. If change is demanded, denial can feel like an elixir. When empathy for ourselves helps us make choices to be responsible, responsibility ceases to be a demand, it becomes a choice. When responsibility is working for us, making us happy, we seriously question irresponsible behaviors. Sometimes we do have to learn a new behavior, but working hard at something that brings obvious positive results is easy to do.

Again, we need to temper working at life with empathy, as there is no end to the progress that can be made. In fact we can take on too much and despair can be the result. How do we know when we're working too hard? We know when we're tired, stressed, or feel like we've just done enough for the time being. We can sense that life offers us infinite possibilities, but only if we take care of ourselves. When we have empathy, we can feel satisfaction with progress and can arrest the pressure of further demands of life.

TRUST

Trust is another big issue that demands clarification from empathy. Like honesty, degrees of trust are broad. Humans rarely do well completely trusting themselves, let alone others, and they don't do well not trusting anyone. When we have empathy for ourselves, we accept we're not perfect, and that likely means that we and others aren't to be perfectly trusted. However, the same level of empathy makes us aware that we do better in relationships, and that relationships feed on trust.

When we use empathy to guide our relationships, we gain a level of trust that will be the greatest determinant of the depth of a relationship. This is another of the workings of a full life: having realistic appraisals of our relationships. Our empathetic relationship with ourselves always needs to be primary, but that doesn't exclude other empathetic relationships.

Like empathy, trust is dynamic. It is both developed and earned. We can quickly learn that it's far easier to lose than to gain. When trust is broken between friends, the incident may be catastrophic or an isolated loss of trust. When we have empathy for our own work in the area of trust, we can even have empathy for broken trust, but that doesn't mean we'll necessarily allow disappointment in the same area of relationship again. When we're not in denial, we take responsibility for being wounded by the same breach of trust a second time.

CONTINUING DEVELOPMENT

As we continue the work of life—essentially accepting limitations and avoiding denial—we continue to develop empathy. Experience is our teacher. When we are in denial, we are easily led on a negative spiral toward despair. With empathy, we can climb the positive steps that support learning. Self-knowledge, when from empathy rather than criticism, is both strong and flexible. It is the basis of personal security.

Security issues are as dynamic as all issues of human development. They include some of the most frightening, and denial-producing, facets of life. We can temper how deep we go into the meaning of life with our level of empathy. Frightening ourselves mercilessly with worries is not empathic. The world itself doesn't exactly feel secure in our global warming nuclear age. Empathy will determine how and how long we can face such issues and remain relatively secure.

Having short-sighted empathy will lead us to denying that we have a life-threatening problem. It's called "indifference" and pretends that there is nothing to be empathic about. Genuine empathy will temper both over-exposure and blindness for what can be done. When we overexpose ourselves to an issue, we're unlikely to think clearly, or at least to remain thinking clearly about that issue. Adequately aware of a threat, we can at least develop concern among others, and perhaps even find a solution.

Global worries where an individual has so little agency need to be dealt with like other traumas. It's called "touch and release." "Touch" is not denying that the worries are genuine. "Release" is not practicing a worry after nothing has been found to do about it. Constant worry without solution is itself a trauma. A genuine worry will be triggered by many common thoughts and events, but, with practice, release leads to a full life.

To expand the harsh statement of Karl Marx, denial is the opiate of the people. He was speaking of religion, but there are many ways to avoid what worries us. Empathy helps us moderate how deeply introspective we can effectively be. Too much exposure to life's uncertainties, when we're already not happy with life, can be damaging, even life threatening. Too little and we risk not seeing a solution to that which excites our insecurity.

At the turn of the nineteenth century, Friedrich Schleiermacher (who was considered one of the first theologians influencing early Protestant religion) stated that the only thing humans actually know about their existence is that they are absolutely dependent. Even in his own time, Schleiermacher wasn't broadly respected. All religions confidently state more than that. Religions all propose that they *know* there is a god.

To think that all we can know about our being is absolute dependence often doesn't satisfy, can frighten, and must be empathetically considered. Absolute dependence can seem to be demeaning of human life. We tend to deny how insignificant we are when compared to natural forces. We can, with appropriate empathy, accept our place in the world and find happiness through our limited agency. The advanced development of the human brain gains us far more possibility than other animals: Our development is far more rapid and expansive.

Adding to the issue raised by Schleiermacher, Karl Jaspers (one of the early existentialists) stated that all reason is rationalization. He didn't mean that all reasoning was a lie, but warned that it could be. With empathy, we can see that the meaning of life is of utmost importance, but it must be understood by working at it, not by rationalization and denial. Some have suggested that just wondering about life without finding personal meaning may have caused the death of another existentialist, Jean-Paul Sartre. Meaning is found in human life by living it, not by wondering about it.

Like rationalization's vulnerability to denial, feelings of accomplishment, and ideologies can be more rigid and even more at risk of denial's corruption. Denial of our rationalizations is a blindness to truth and reality. It often leads to defensiveness, which may be a sign that we're not comfortable with our half-truths and outright lying to ourselves. The truth really does set us free. Free to see the counterintuitive, the drawbacks, and the negative possibilities.

Looking at anything that we've done well, from a social skill to something we've created, accomplishment provides happiness. Yes, self-improvement can be a waste of time, but only if we use it without empathy. When we have time, maturation feels like meaning and purpose. Worrying about existence may be interesting to some, but is only marginally relevant to finding personal happiness. Empathy doesn't just help us adjust to life; it provides meaning.

When we combine empathy with exposure to meaning-of-life issues, they become a part of our security and don't require denial. There are many things to be afraid of in this world, and that affect our security. With freedom from denial, and empathy for ourselves, fear can help us check the house for bad wiring, but it can't do much if we fear an asteroid destroying our planet. Empathy hurries our approach to bad wiring and limits our concerns about asteroids.

When life is going well, the concept of absolute dependency can be useful in limiting our arrogance. Humility fits human growth far better than arrogance.

If we have a concept of a creator of our existence, then we can see our lives as an evolutionary process. Our potential for applying lessons from mistakes for continual growth, makes it difficult to think that we're dependent on something that's negative.

Evolution is about improved adaptation, which suggests that failures are just a part of a positive process. Such a rationalization may not be true, but is easy to believe when not in denial. Knowing that we could rationalize solutions to life is a basic protection against allowing denial to limit our progress.

Empathy brings the gift of confidence without arrogance. We've earned our confidence. We have pride in our work, but we're not prideful. We're living well. Of course, that doesn't mean living without pain. We are still easily hurt. Perhaps more so in that we're less defended. But we remain confident in our struggle with life. We remain empathic towards ourselves and others. Our pain becomes the basis of empathy for the pain of others.

When life becomes fascinating in all of its complexity, we're free to wonder. Is there something beyond this life? Can societies mature? Can war be ended? What more is there for us to do with ourselves? The life lived well is never boring and leaves no regrets. When we like our progress, we have no regrets. Our empathy has matured into a behavior and a tool for guiding our success. And, success has become a process, not a goal.

We easily forget that humans are evolving in this world just like plants and other animals. Evolution obviously doesn't mean that we'll survive, but it does mean that we can adapt. Empathy can both motivate and lead us in this evolutionary process of adaptation and survival.

STEPS THAT MAY DEEPEN UNDERSTANDING:

1. Reflect on how much empathy you have received from others and how it's affected you.

2. Think about loving yourself as not necessarily narcissistic.

3. Consider the role of empathy in the behavior of forgiveness.

4. Compare empathy for yourself and others with having empathy for the behaviors of young children. It's easy to know they have a lot to learn, and aren't responsible for mistakes that are behaviors beyond their abilities.

5. Look at how you have or haven't developed a strong sense of empathy.

Could a greater miracle take place
than for us to look through
each other's eyes for an instant?

Henry David Thoreau

Chapter Eight
PATIENCE, PERSEVERANCE, AND PROGRESS

There is no quick fix for overcoming denial. In this fast-paced world, the most challenging part is accepting that changing a negative habit can take years. Depending on when we start, we may never feel "fixed," but we can find a good deal of happiness in making progress. Our lives won't feel so out of control. We can avoid the despair of feeling stuck, unchangeable.

We usually need to develop our understanding of these following key elements for successful living: patience, perseverance, and progress. There is recent evidence that patience and perseverance, like other aspects of personality, have a neurological origin. They are neurologically developed without much effort on our parts in early childhood if we have adequate caregivers. Fortunately, like other aspects of our personalities, they can also be developed in adulthood.

Working memory plays an important part when we need to work on patience and perseverance as adults.

197

Working memory is described as parts of memory that are available in current thinking and easily retrievable. Results from recent research on irritable mothers showed that, when the mothers were able to quickly remember—like what to expect of a young child— then they were able to inhibit being irritable with them. One of the related issues being discovered is that working memory often becomes tied up by stress, distraction, and issues like worrying about being a bad mother.

Thus, if we're to develop patience and perseverance as adults, we also need to have developed empathy, critical thinking, rules, and all the issues the prior chapters have discussed. Free of fear and labelling, our working memory can develop a defense for our impatience and help us persevere even when a change is taking a long time. Accepting that we tend to be impatient is crucially different from harboring negative labels that easily defeat our perseverance.

THE STRUGGLE FOR CHANGE

Once we accept that we have a behavior we'd like to change, a struggle begins. It may sound surprising, but the more imminent the damage to ourselves from practicing our habit, the easiest it is to change. However, such habits are only the easiest if we don't give up right away in frustration. Fatal habits like smoking, drug addictions, and poor eating choices, can remain in our neurological connections most because of the high first-attempt failure rate. When we break through our initial denial, patience and perseverance are aided by the lethality of the habit. Then we're more likely to make progress.

Denial can even obscure us from determining that we'd like to change a habit. We lie to ourselves about the human ability to change and the risk-trajectory of the behavior. Basically, after trying to change any remarkable behavior, it's easy to give up all attempts and make excuses and inaccurate explanations. As we discussed in Chapter Three, the very idea of trying can be misleading; in essence, we aren't quitting, we're trying. Then we can soon fall into indifference or even despair as our excuse.

When we don't succeed at a change, we need to try and try again. However, like the little train that could, we need to think we can, and stay on track. Trying is but a frustration when we don't have realistic expectations, when we don't have understanding of the issues we're confronting and solutions for them. Failure with initial trying then ties up the working memory we need for strategies of long-term change.

When we've given up, we've misled ourselves with misinformation. Perhaps we know people who smoked and drank heavily but yet died in old age. Possibly we've said the problem is in our genes, and nothing can be done about that. Sometimes we may have even thought, *Who wants to live anyway?* Perhaps our lack of mathematical understanding and probability data are part of the problem, but when we are honest with ourselves, we can still understand the risk of thinking of ourselves as an exception.

Even when our excuse is that we don't want to live anyway, denial keeps us from being honest about the negative effects our behaviors on others, and the diminished conditions of living before we die. Like most unfixed problems, what was a nuisance too often becomes a crisis. The suggestion to cheer up as things could be worse takes on an important meaning at this point. Often our negative habit is about cheering us up, and things do get worse.

We have many ways to cheer ourselves up that don't work over time and most often exacerbate the problem: Drinking alcohol, eating poorly, using prescription drugs, and engaging in unhealthy sex are common. They all can stem from avoidance. They all can be examples of denial. The blindness of denial alone damages our lives by allowing us to buy time for problems to get worse, usually with physical consequences.

FIRST STEPS

When we understand the potential damage from using denial for the wrong issues in our lives, we can take important steps. As we've already discussed, the first is acceptance that we have a particularly important problem behavior. Then we need to make ourselves aware of our fears, set some rules for overcoming habituation, and develop empathy for ourselves. After that, we still need patience.

A well-developed working memory gives us a chance to remember things that can limit our frustration. Then we can be more patient with ourselves when we're trying to change a well-practiced behavior. We are just repeating such behaviors from habit; the behaviors themselves are not trying to frustrate us. If we don't immediately recognize this in our working memory, we need to take more time to consciously remember.

Understanding is the basic element of patience. Even those of us with slow working memory can usually find ways to take time for understanding. When we understand that most behaviors, like those of an infant, aren't under conscious control, we can be patient—as long as we protect ourselves from being hurt by the behaviors. For example, when we understand that arrogant people are usually protecting an insecurity, we can be patient with them. We may move away from them, but we are less likely to react negatively towards them.

Being patient with ourselves is perhaps the most difficult. It's difficult, and dangerous, to move away from ourselves. It's an issue of being true to our best self, not our bad habits. Here, patience helps us understand, and understanding helps us be patient. It's a win-win situation. Obviously, patience needs to be developed if we haven't yet advanced our understanding. Patience must also be partnered with awareness. Without enough patience at this early stage of behavior, frustration and even anger may easily cloud our efforts at changing our thinking.

Ironically, understanding needs to be an intellectual discipline before patience if we don't have the patience for understanding. That's when reading and other intellectual endeavors are useful. It will feel artificial when we develop patience because we've accepted that we lack this ability, but it will work. It's the *fake it 'till you make it* plan. When we feel frustrated or angry, we can recognize that such feelings won't be helpful, and we can try more deeply to understand just what our situation is, and why it's frustrating. Then we can find the patience we need.

One warning: We can be too patient. With others, we may put up with too much and not move away. With ourselves, we can lose the impetus for change if we're too patient. Balance in such things is a crucial mental behavior for us to have well developed. With a developed ability to balance needs in our lives, patience will be effective for our needed changes. This balance may be another of the first behaviors we need to focus on if we're to progress.

ROLE OF UNDERSTANDING

When we develop understanding for how difficult it is for humans to make changes to their lives, we will effectively develop patience for our difficulty with negative behaviors. We change all our lives, but that's a different type of change. We express genes, change our biology, physically and psychologically develop the ability to learn, develop muscle, and, in many but not all ways, deteriorate in old age. But changing habits that we've inappropriately learned consistently requires much patience.

As we've seen in prior chapters, behaviors like unsafe driving practices or unhealthy eating habits are as set in our neurological system as the behavior of breathing. When we get a warning that a behavior is harmful, we need to be patient with ourselves, not the behavior. We need to learn to be impatient with poor and sometimes dangerous practices, while being patient with our struggle in changing entrenched behaviors. When we don't understand this rule, we easily despair regarding change and accept harmful behaviors.

Behavior is always supported by unconscious mechanisms in the brain. Dealing with conscious change of unconsciously supported behaviors is a struggle with abstract concepts, but it doesn't take an advanced intelligence. Change is basically simple once we know we can succeed and develop patience for our ability to do it. As noted in Chapter Six, we have to develop and follow some rules.

For illustration, a most obvious rule would be to keep no secrets about having sexual affairs, or robbing banks for that matter. Perhaps not as obvious, making a rule to clearly state, even if just to our self, why we're going to have an alcoholic drink can awaken change.

If our answer is, for example, that being intoxicated is the only time we're happy, we have a good chance of finding a healthier way to be happy.

Of course, the ability to find better ways assumes that we aren't despairing about making changes. Many of our secrets hide in the face of denial. We are rarely happy with behaviors that we do in secret. Shame can easily encourage denial that we are even using secrets to protect a poorly conceived behavior. Awareness involves thinking honestly—the opposite of denial—and requires patience to completely understand this issue.

It's important to notice that changes are rarely easy. Behaviors are usually interconnected with other behaviors and one change can trigger a change in another situation. Let's say we recognize that we're not happy in a major personal or business relationship. Making a change from such a relationship usually leads to several other, potentially frightening changes. They all may have positive solutions, but not if our fear leads to denying the necessary critical thinking.

When we don't make changes, we can protect the behavior more and more and it can become more automatic in our unconscious system. Like recognizing when we need to eat or breath, the behavior we want to change can re-emerge automatically. With patience, we can train our brain that the behavior is a mistake. Self-talk can keep us focused on our desire to change something, especially if our words are patient and understanding, not demeaning.

We easily anthropomorphize the workings of our unconscious mind. We call it clever, out to get us, or even evil. When we externalize our unconscious mind in such a way, our issue can gain power. Such name calling is a product of our frustration, but also a clever denial of our power to change. It can make patience more difficult to practice. We need to believe in our ability to change to maintain consistent patience with ourselves.

THE BEST STARTING PLACE

The situation isn't a catch-22: namely, we need belief that we can change before we can make the changes that bring the belief. We can all make changes if we start small, and build on the skill until we clearly feel belief in our ability. It may be hard on our ego to start small, but such a test needs to sound reasonable. Surely we can make a simple rule, like just to notice a behavior. Such a rule should be about a single event, not several bad habits at once.

Success is unlikely if we first try to change a behavior that is likely to happen throughout the day. Denial will surely win. But, many of us can limit one isolated behavior if we choose carefully. The rule needs to be carefully formulated, often reformulated after it doesn't succeed, as just repeating the try is usually unsuccessful. It truly needs to be simple at first as success is important and adequate patience may not be developed well enough.

Trying not to pick your nose, swear, eat too much, and the like, are usually not good choices. Success is more likely in dealing with issues like sharing a household task such as taking the garbage out once a week. This is a single event. For example, let's say we decide that we will take it out each week for a while. Then we forget. Seeing the situation as a test that may take time and reason, we can develop a rule. We may decide on something like placing the car keys in an envelope on which is written the words "Garbage Day?"

Such a solution may sound simple, but denial can still delay success. We'll need to remember that developing patience depends on success with simple tests, and that accepting it might take reason and time. We might, for example, decide that a rule is too strict, or that we can drop it after initial success. When we keep at this change in behavior—taking the garbage out consistently, for example—we will recognize that the harder a task is to accomplish, the more understanding we will gain about personal change and denial.

Success at one relatively simple change may not lead to believing we can then stop a hugely negative behavior, but it will help us develop patience, make us feel a little more hopeful, and may impress a partner or friend to be more supportive of our willingness to change. When we have some hope, patience, and support, we may feel less frightened to recognize our part in the unhappinesses we experience. We might even take pleasure in finding that we can exercise some control over ourselves.

We too often try to control our world rather than ourselves. Changing others is usually more difficult. If only he would be more thoughtful. If I wasn't in such a stressful situation. If my friends didn't drink so much. If the government would just stay out of the free-market. Trying to control behaviors other than our own easily becomes a trick of denial distracting us from change we can control. When denial supports failure we easily get caught up in hopelessness, whereas even a small success controlling ourselves develops hopefulness.

After we have a little hope, and a smattering of patience, perseverance comes into play. We are so used to fast food and quick fixes that we may feel lost on the road ahead. On this journey toward a fuller happiness, for perseverance we need to look down the road, but our focus needs to be more on the mile markers as opposed to the horizon. Taking too much on our plate can lead to more problems than obesity.

To persevere, we need to make the most of setbacks, make changes in our plans, and maintain a focus on the program of beating denial. We need to be steadfast in this pursuit, faithful to our purpose. With progress we are likely to find a different meaning in life than we've perceived before: becoming more human. When we persevere, other elements of our life may fall secondary, but will quickly benefit from our pursuits.

We often attach the goal of being the best person we can be to a person, a job, or an objective to the neglect of making real changes in our life. Cranking out success with work at specific times of our life can be rewarding, but can leave us quite vulnerable to failure that may deeply surprise us. Despair is often the result. Finding meaning in life isn't about external successes. Again, it's about making progress as a human being.

We can become an important person at work, feel good about our standard of living, even take pride in our service to the world, but it's not as important as feeling that we can change when we want to improve on some behavior. We can easily feel stuck when we seem to have many signs of success in life. Behaviors like comparison and competition can still be deadly, literally. Maslow's research on factors of well-being supports my feelings about the importance of feeling control.

COMMITTED TO PROGRESS

Perseverance, when supported by success and the resulting hope, is about finding denial at play in our lives. It's about being more aware, even when it hurts. Winning battles with denial gives us a sense of confidence. With enough success in this struggle, fear is more easily overcome. Then, self-appraisal, that commonly missing element needed for personal growth, is clearer and more present.

Learning to persevere doesn't mean life gets easy. Change is usually work. The value of the work, once apparent, does make perseverance easier. Giving up usually has to do with thinking we won't succeed.

Even when we're successful in our external pursuits, we can feel stuck, even bored. Human potential is one of the pursuits of life where we can't top out. We'll rarely feel that life is too easy.

With patience and perseverance on this journey of life, we make progress. Again, progress is an essential ingredient in personal happiness. It wouldn't be wise to think that we have full control over our lives—we barely influence government even if we vote and contribute, and even if we get elected, and an individual can't solve world problems like war and poverty in a lifetime—but patience and perseverance are the places where we have the most control.

That doesn't mean we can forget the broader problems. One of the aspects of our lives that we all benefit from, when we're able to develop it, is empathy. When people of the world have developed enough empathy, more of our resources will be used to solve our huge human problems. But, as discussed in Chapter Seven, developing empathy is personal work, and takes time.

As we develop, it doesn't always feel like work, but it always takes time. When we commit to a fuller life, growth feels natural, but we will still need patience and perseverance. The commitment is to our evolution. It's like a good partnership. A commitment to a relationship between two people sees them through the rough times that are eventually considered a growth process. If they have many behaviors of love between them, then mistakes won't likely ruin the relationship.

When we have understanding of the human process supported by consistent loving behaviors, we won't have any judgmentalism, and fear will be diminished. Fear is the primary enemy of perseverance. Even when others judge us without understanding, if we're making progress with our patience and perseverance, then we can remain hopeful and continue in our progress.

Like so many elements of our lives, denial can corrupt our progress. Unlike many other areas where we can make progress, we miss the meaning of our human evolution if we accept progress as enough. Progress may be a key to our happiness, but we won't understand the meaning of human life if we accept a certain achievement as enough, as an end-point.

Like the rest of creation, humans are always evolving. When we forget our place in the evolution of the beings on our planet, we should suspect denial. With evolution, there is no end-point. Creation is on-going, limitless. Finding that we can change our behaviors should excite us with possibility. We will likely easily find more to do after each success as we will have overcome denial once more, gained more hope, and will be less likely to fear a next step for developing our human potential.

As with accomplishment, progress needs to be understood as a gift rewarding our patience and perseverance on the journey of life. If we consider progress with a negative behavior as good enough, we are in danger of relapse and discouragement, the loss of hope. Pride in an unfinished status quo is only safe when we stay on the journey. An example is an alcoholic who has stopped drinking and its associate behaviors, but who is still miserable and is in denial of what more is possible.

Having pride in a life unfinished subjects us to despair. We may be better in some way, but are still causing ourselves or others disappointment, or even pain. We will never be finished with our evolution in this life. If we stop growing, we may feel the need to let denial reign again. Looking at our unfinished changes without hope of making further change can weaken our resolve and strengthen our despair.

This is why we're often surprised that major accomplishments never feel like enough. When this surprise disappoints us, we can find that we were working for a prize instead of a life-goal—if we're not in denial, that is. Having denial is not believing in life. It arises out of our fear that we aren't successful. This successfulness isn't what life is about. Really living is making progress. Progress is genuine successfulness. Anything less is like trying to fill a pot that has a hole in it.

Failure is frightening when we are pursuing success, but is only a lesson when we're just progressing on our life-journey. Failure still hurts, but the pain is ameliorated by the awareness of growth. Failure can be terminal when we pursue goals other than living. We can lose sight of goals by making mistakes. Life is only lost in death. Goals can motivate us, but they aren't progress. Living is progress.

LIFE AS JOURNEY

Evolving into the best human we can be needs to be our central goal. Each one of us has a unique journey. We don't know how far we'll get, how long we have. As we develop, we learn about our damage and our beauty: Each of us damaged in our own history, and uniquely beautiful in our progress.

Seeing life as development ties us to creation. We can then feel oneness with the rest of reality. The neocortex, the newest development in the brains of mammals, is dramatically more developed in humans. In terms of size relative to the rest of the brain, only elephants and dolphins even come close. It's important for us to remember that we're still learning to use it. Our dominance over other animals may be a source of our arrogance, which has become a threat to our very existence.

Unlike arrogance, gaining a sense of ourselves as unfinished supports being patient, persevering, and finding joy in progress. An evolutionary understanding of humans might also help us with issues like anger, discrimination, and judgmentalism. Any comparison of differences between us needs to be about skill levels and other issues on the surface of life. And comparison that neglects personal histories is crucially flawed.

Enthusiasm for Thomas Harris's book *I'm OK—You're OK* quickly diminished in the early seventies. The good feeling the title gave us just didn't hold up. If being OK is about making progress, and not settling for complacency, then it doesn't aid denial. If not feeling okay leads to despair, then denial will support our lack of awareness. When we're thinking clearly, we recognize that all humans are works in progress. Both feeling okay and not okay can contribute to any progress.

Humans are fine creations. However, without developing wisdom about how we develop, we tend to repeat mistakes. Denial plays an important role in our repeated negative behaviors. It's so pervasive that many of us may think that we can't overcome denial. Our ability to make progress as humans is frequently obscured by using denial in just that way.

But once we appreciate who we are, more than what we accomplish, we can envision a beautiful life. Progress is a beauty that can exist in the midst of a sea of ugly mistakes. It's available to all. It's how our brain works. We don't have to become scientists to develop our lives, just awareness. Awareness, strengthened by hope if not belief, is all we need to pursue happiness through progress.

STEPS THAT MAY DEEPEN UNDERSTANDING.

1. Notice that patience requires understanding. There are many situations like the patience one gains by having developmentally appropriate expectations of children.

2. If you lack what you consider to be success, consider how small steps can be important. There are likely to be many small steps by which you will experience success.

3. Notice how success is critical to having hope. Have you ignored success—thus not benefitting from it—because the task seemed too trivial?

4. Consider how hope is crucial for perseverance. Think about anything you gave up on: Was it fear supported by a lack of hope for success.

5. Reflect on how progress produces happiness, not just goal achievement.

The best way
to make your dreams come true
is to wake up.

Paul Valery

Chapter Nine
DENIAL AND
AUTHORITARIANISM

We cannot afford to be in denial about the authoritarian world in which most of us live. The industrial world has accidently destroyed the authoritative world of tribal villages from which we all once came. Briefly defined, authoritarian operates with demands and punishments, whereas authoritative functions using minding, modeling, and mentoring. All of the elements needed for winning a battle against the denial that cages us in a too-limited world are easily weakened, even destroyed, by authoritarianism.

Even if our parents weren't authoritarian, our schools and employment situations are commonly authoritarian. When we don't have superior personal security, teachers and employers can easily make us feel less than we are. The development of self-esteem meaning, control and belonging, as described by Abraham Maslow, all suffer in a demand-and-punish world. Authoritarianism is judgmental by design.

Worst of all, it leads to being judgmental about ourselves.

Judgment wouldn't be so devastating if it was used to address our behavior, but a person is rarely separated from his or her behavior. Even wisely separated, receivers of negative judgment of their behavior have difficulty separating the criticism to understand that the judgment does not mean there's something specifically wrong with them. Red ink on a math paper or an essay can easily be understood as meaning the person is "less-than." The feeling can be especially strong if we aren't mentored into understanding that the correction simply gives direction about the need for improvement.

In an authoritarian world we easily end up feeling stupid about math, language, computers, or many issues, and that diminishes our self-worth. When we feel diminished, we often pretend to be all right. Feeling less-than feels like not-belonging in a society that pretends to be all right. In the authoritarian world, it's crucial to understand that many people are pretending. Then we can be aware that not being perfect is normal. That should help with a major cause of our denial.

Many of our human models in the industrialized world are pretenders who don't have our best interest at heart, and even mentor in an authoritarian style. We need to recognize that authoritarianism can easily be judgmental, and the judgmentalism easily leads to ostracism. That's not effective for society, let alone for us. Ostracism turns the four elements of human happiness that Maslow helped us understand into alienation, meaninglessness, helplessness, and worthlessness. Denial often feels necessary when we're reduced to such feelings of despair.

When we become accustomed to the ostracism inherent in authoritarianism, it is difficult to accept our responsibility for, let alone tragedies resulting from, our failures. We can learn much from an eight-year-old who suffered sexual abuse at the hands of her father's corrupted love. She demanded to take some of the responsibility for him being in prison. She told of a friend who suggested she should have just said no to her father when he wanted to touch her inappropriately.

When allowed even 5 percent of the responsibility, she finished her treatment sooner than most. We might all do better if we weren't afraid of accepting our responsibility for our difficulties. We've already discussed that blaming ourselves or others is little help for finding success after suffering failures, but being in denial about our part in a failure is counterproductive. Accepting some responsibility for our behavior doesn't mean we accept blame; however, accepting responsibility allows us to take some control over future behaviors.

When we are made to feel helpless, we are usually denying our ability to educate ourselves about the skills needed for successful living. All too common, we take how we live as a given, something we can do little about. We may think we already know enough about living our lives, and that we can learn nothing more of any significance. However, sometimes the problem is that we've searched in the wrong places for more education about living skills, or we didn't know how difficult using such information is.

When we think we can't learn enough to change our lives, we feel stuck, of course, and even helpless. The effect of ostracism is even stronger when it comes from within. Personal change isn't fast or easy, but it is possible. We have all experienced many events that were out of our control, and that caused personal failure, including those that made us feel helpless. Not denying the many causes of failure will help us turn blame into hope. Considering what we can learn about failure can help us understand some of the challenges to living well that all humans experience, and even help us make healthy changes in our lives.

When we aren't aware of the challenges set in placed for us by authoritarian parenting or education in our childhoods, it's difficult not to blame ourselves for a lack of happiness. Self-blame is difficult to take, day in and day out, so we usually develop defenses: blaming others, believing in bad luck, and even believing in unreasonable optimism about our future. These ares some of the many forms of denial.

When we try to educate ourselves about our condition, we may look to pop-psychology that suggests easy steps for success. But easy isn't known to provide long-term success. What has been found to be more successful is to do the hard work of better self-appraisal, and stepping out of denial. Denial damages, even eliminates, our self-appraisal, our understanding of our part in things that go wrong.

Adequate self-appraisal is clearly one of the first lessons to learn if we are to overcome the effects of authoritarianism, and make progress toward happiness. However, society offers little support for acknowledging our failures and their causes. We far more often judge ourselves and others, which limits our acceptance of how humans naturally make mistakes. Happiness requires that we accept our mistakes, be as aware of them as we can, and learn from them. Denied, our mistakes drag us down. Recognized and accepted, any negative aspects of our childhood help us avoid this tragic denial. Effective self-appraisal is at the core of developing our self-esteem, and our sense of control over our lives.

Feeling that no one cares for us is a common result of attitudes regarding our mistakes. In denial of how we didn't learn effective living skills, and how can still learn them, our defenses easily give way to judgmental attitudes about ourselves. This negative self-appraisal assists one's feelings of not being cared for, which is usually the main thing missing in a suicidal person's life.

Not feeling cared for is a complex issue. This doesn't necessarily mean these people weren't cared for; sometimes people's ability to receive and understand love behaviors of others has been corrupted. For example, much can go wrong in childhood that sets adolescents against their caregivers' love. Such problems can start as early as infancy, when a caregiver may have found caring for us difficult.

Although feeling cared for is important, as are other needs, feeling like we're in control of our life is crucial. Even feeling abandoned and useless wouldn't be so extreme if we knew we could do something about it. Pain is usually manageable; what is unbearable is feeling that we're stuck with that pain. When we believe we're unable to change a painful life situation, ending life can make sense to us. Many survive by just feeling indifferent about their despair. That can feel like effective denial, but breaks down when trouble accumulates in the fog of such thinking.

WELL-INFORMED RESPONSIBILITY

Central to allowing authoritarianism to make us feel helpless is an issue of feeling completely responsible for our lives. We often don't understand the things we may have missed as our personalities are developed. Then, when life falls apart in some way, we can feel that it's entirely our failure and that we can do nothing about it. At that point, many see suicide as an almost responsible thing to do. It's at least *something* we feel we can do. Too many people commit suicide, but the majority of us continue suffering in such a situation, pretending that we're all right.

Rarely considered is how unconsciously programmed our personality and behaviors are. Our personality has a great deal to do with how successful we are at living. When we experience success, as a child or as an adult, we feel some control over our lives. Control leads to more success, and more success leads to feelings of belonging and worthwhileness. That's a good cycle. Experiencing repeated failure in an authoritarian world can feel more like a black hole drawing us into oblivion.

If we can understand that causes beyond our control set us on such a path of frustration and failure, we may be able to take a new path. As with starting anything new, we'll have to educate ourselves. The journey needs to start with accepting that we had an inadequate start, that we may have missed the information needed to be a successful person. Discovering the damage that mistakes in our childhood easily set off helps us know where to start looking for helpful information.

In the beginning denial is easily supported, especially in this authoritarian/judgmental society, as we can have difficulty discerning between blaming our parents and blaming their behaviors. It's important to make this distinction though. When not separated, it can become easy to continue denial, especially at the crucial moment of contemplating suicide. We need to understand that our parents also lived in an authoritarian world, where asking how to parent better would have been admitting mistakes—a difficult thing to do in a world where everyone is pretending to be doing well.

When we consider that the powerful aspects of personality that help us find happiness are developed by life experiences, many of them in our pre-school years, then we easily see how happiness can elude us if we do not develop these aspects properly. However, we can develop a sense of having independent personal control over our life-success in adulthood.

Many elements of life can make us feel helpless, unable to control our lives. In domestic violence situations, the element is called "learned helplessness." It may be good to use this term more broadly. When we don't know that we can change our personalities, we have essentially learned to be helpless. Usually we learned this helplessness by trying to change in ineffective ways, wrongly learning—or unfortunately believing—that we're inadequate.

Denying that we feel inadequate can lead to incredible negative behaviors, including further denial regarding other issues. Denial after denial can easily obliterate the road back to reality. Like depression, feeling inadequacy is only an end-of-life problem when we also don't feel any control, which can result from a lack of self-esteem regarding success with change.

THE ROLE OF PERSONALITY

We are seeing that it's easy for individuals to feel like their lives are an impossible mess. Our personalities are initially shaped mostly by others—our parents, caregivers, teachers, etc. Our sense of security, intelligence, and much else was constantly shaped by experiences with others. When we get to know another person, it would be rare to find that their personality is very close to being perfectly functional. It's important to know that we often make the challenges of living worse when we don't understand our limitations, and haven't adequately learned how to address them.

It often feels easier to quit than to try to understand what holds us back from happiness. We leave relationships, employment, and other situations without assessing if changes are possible on our part. We compound the issue by denying that there is something to learn about ourselves if we're to do better the next time we enter a relationship.

We cannot quickly change our personalities by attending a lecture, reading a book, finding new friends, or other resources. It usually takes years to change an unconscious habit that is deeply embedded in our daily lives, and many habits form our personalities. Our minds have many ways to bring us back to behaviors we've long practiced. It's not a bad system. As we've already noted, such practice literally makes breathing easy, and can lead to complex skills like playing a musical instrument.

Our challenge can be compounded by having few models for effective change. We read about current diets failing, attempts to reduce poverty failing, and treatments for addictions not working well. Living effectively is work, and we rarely hear that. It takes time to learn how to do it, and the steps must include reducing denial.

Accepting our limitations is difficult, at times even scary. Goethe is known to have said something about how if he knew himself, he would run away. Blaming ourselves and others is far easier. It does little good to decide that our caregivers let us down, that our teachers weren't adequate, that employers are often mean, and that many others affecting our lives offer negative experiences. Though important to recognize such behaviors that affected us negatively, it's not wise to dwell on them.

Our focus needs to be on finding and working with the limitations that are in the way of effective living. Acceptance of causes of our disappointments without blaming is the self-appraisal so necessary for positive change. Patience will be needed, but acceptance develops insights into new strategies. Insight can be as simple as slowing down behaviors, including speech, to test the possible consequences.

Without accepting that we've had personal limitations placed in our lives, we tend to either bluff that we're all right or struggle silently with feelings of helplessness. It is crucial that we accept how we are without accepting that our condition is who we are. Personal education makes the difference between being stuck and finding ways to change our situation. All of creation changes over thousands of years; humans can significantly change in a lifetime.

We can only find enough success for happiness by discovering that it is up to us to learn the effective skills of adult living. As noted previously, it's also crucial to recognize that happiness doesn't necessarily come with money or accomplishment. Happiness is more likely to come from feeling good about ourselves. Finding we can learn from errors, and being patient about having made them, can lead us to feeling in control of our many life experiences, and then feeling good about ourselves.

When we don't know that we can learn much as an adult on the road to happiness, helplessness can easily defeat us. If we haven't developed a sense of control over our lives in adulthood, we're likely to take comfort in denial, or even suicidal ideation. If we're to learn about the work of living effectively, we need to consider both what we've learned that is undermining our attempts, and also what we didn't learn that would bring us success.

Looking at what is necessary for healthy development can help us understand both what we missed, and help us with the knowledge and motivation for developing control in our lives. If we set out to do any job without education regarding the skills and knowledge needed to accomplish the tasks well, we might not be surprised if success evades us. Living is like employment, with many layers of complex tasks, and we're often not well prepared them.

Sometimes we're also well trained in expecting too much of ourselves, and for taking the blame for any deficits. Then we're in trouble with what we believe is expected of us in life. If we also have a poorly developed sense of agency (control), we might have trouble learning from our mistakes. Trial and error doesn't work if we blame instead of pay attention, and it's hard to pay attention when we don't feel a sense of control over our responses to life's situations.

EARLY CHILDHOOD EFFECTS

How much control can we have over our social skills, our personality? Recently, genetics has been consistently seen as roughly two-thirds responsible for our functioning as humans. Current genetic information even suggests that our DNA at birth determines how easily we are cared for. A third of us are basically comfortable, flexible in our attitude, and easy to care for as infants. The rest of us are withdrawn or anxious, and our caregivers are required to do more to guide us well.

Genes control our biology and some of our behaviors throughout life, but which genes find expression will be more dependent on what happens in our environment. For example, the source of developmental disabilities may be found in our chromosomes, but how we're treated will make substantial differences in how we develop. Our genetic inheritance will make problems like obesity and drug abuse more likely, but won't make them a certainty.

The nature-nurture controversy is no longer argued in psychological science. They are both seen as responsible for our behaviors. Both genes and how our caregivers tend to us as infants greatly determine how our personalities form. By the end of our first year, we can be characterized as being withdrawn, anxious, or secure about learning life's lessons. By two years of age personality is difficult to change. Many behaviors, effective and dysfunctional, follow this beginning.

These basic personality issues are found at birth and have been researched as attachment styles by Mary Ainsworth. Following up on John Bowlby's theories, she tested for the effects of a mother's interactions in her child's first year of life. Geneticists have used her attachment-vocabulary to describe these at-birth personality styles. It isn't clear where researched attachment issues in the first year of life fits in this new genetic picture.

The research of Ainsworth, and now many others, is unlikely to be disregarded, but will have to be integrated with these findings regarding personality at birth. It may be that even if we were, for instance, born anxious, we can have a secure attachment style before we're two years old. Developing changes in attachment depends on whether or not our caregivers are up to the challenge. Then again, even a secure child can be a problem as they try more things, and may be more trouble for caregivers than those who end up having a withdrawn or anxious style of personality.

It is important that caregivers understand the child's testing of situations as another important lesson about the work of life. If caregivers use an authoritarian approach to control such children, the children won't learn much about controlling themselves. Toddlers don't deserve the labeling phrase of "terrible twos"; they are just learning about their environment. Children can feel totally in charge as infants, making demands of caregivers, and then see that there's more to life. That's when they have to adjust to the wisdom and power of caregivers.

It's clear that a great deal of our knowledge about how to live successfully can be learned early on, and that not gaining this knowledge can set us up for despair. Further, much more can go well, or go wrong, in the next three years. Many of these developmental theories have been researched only in the past decade. Many caregivers have been and continue to be unaware that the early years are so important.

As adults, it's up to us to know that acceptance of our condition is all-important. Acceptance provides us with the ability to change our personality and related behaviors. A lack of self-appraisal without blame can cause us to repeat failures. Again, it's clear that fear, and a lack of acceptance, or change, can drive denial.

We need to assess and accept our pre-school years if we are to stop blaming ourselves, or to stop feeling worthless and helpless. We're our needs met quickly? The response time to an infant's cries appears as important to the development of a personality as our genetic predisposition. A consistent delay of just a few minutes can apparently cause the development of an anxious or withdrawn style of personality.

Were our emotions soothed? The world is a scary place for young children, especially without trusted people to help them feel safe. A calm face, a relaxed body, and soothing words go a long way to comfort children and encourage a willingness in them to explore the things they're experiencing. How many of us had such caregivers consistently available to us when we needed them?

Were the stages of our development understood so our mistakes weren't dealt with harshly? For example, when a two-year-old knocks over the TV while exploring, is he understood, or yelled at? As children, were we inhibited from exploring by fear, and thus unable to learn many lessons that would later be quite important? Two-year-olds are learning that they aren't the masters of their world. With careful guidance, they can also learn how to take a successful place in it.

Did our caregivers talk and read to us enough to help us develop thousands of words? Preschool children need words to think, understand, regulate their emotions, and develop social skills. Many children go to the first grade with less than 6,000 words in their vocabulary. That's not enough for school success. Some children have more than 20,000 words by that time. Without adequate words for cognition, emotions, behaviors, and social skills can't be well developed.

It has been found that children who eat with their family, even two times a week, with the TV off, have a significantly higher rate of high school graduation than those who do not share this time. Conversation provides children the words they need to develop clear thinking. Without reading and conversation at home, children go to school without enough words to understand what's expected of them.

Emotional regulation is another excellent example of the effects of having enough words for adequate thinking. When children have adequate words to describe their emotions, they have been found to be more able to learn to control their emotions. If children do not learn to regulate emotions in childhood, they will have much more difficulty controlling them as adults. It doesn't take much experience to know that adults who haven't developed the ability to adequately control their emotions achieve less success in life. Emotions can be restrained in an authoritarian situation, but aren't effectively developed by demand and punish.

When a child can use words for cognitions about emotional regulation and effective behaviors, they are developing social skills. Social skills have been found to be more important for school and life success than a person's level of general intelligence. Social skills, adequate sleep, and good nutrition are the primary requirement for success in elementary school according to surveys of teachers. Studies have supported that these three aspects of successful living are important throughout our life cycle.

Faked social skills work sometimes, but are difficult to sustain and are often seen through. Genuine social skills are about generosity, empathy, productivity, and several basic elements of personality, not just about "please," and "thank you." They work because they're appreciated in relationships including those with educators. Well practiced, social skills also help us learn new information by feeling engagement with a subject.

We sometimes forget that rational regulation also needs to be learned. Such a strength of personality isn't directly developed until the teenage years, but its precursors are started as early as two years of age. Rational regulation is necessary to avoid denial in adult life, and is much easier to learn if the most critical precursor of emotional regulation has been learned. A work ethic, critical thinking, and perseverance depend on emotional regulation.

When we don't understand powerful childhood events, self-blame is a natural response. For example, did we eat salt, sweets, and fats too early, changing our stomach chemistry? Such changes have been found to set us up for obesity and all of its physical and mental health risks. Further, in a world of individual responsibility, obesity usually is accompanied by blame from self and others. Obesity can be overcome with years of intense discipline, but we need to approach this free of blame and driven by a wisdom that many of us don't have.

Such wisdom usually comes when we're preschoolers if we've learned that thinking frees us from fear of the unknown. Our early thinking helps us to be more secure as we come to understand more and more of the constantly strange elements of the greatly unknown world of a child. When we understand more, we are less frightened, less frightened, we understand more. This is a positive circle of mental wellness, but many of us are left out of the loop.

Many children are aggressive when they find the world to be frightening. Of course, a lack of sleep or other discomfort will do that to all of us, but when aggression is used as a response to fright, it disrupts solutions. Some children withdraw when frightened, and that disrupts solutions for living as well. How many of us aren't prepared for issues we face as adults due to a lack of learned solutions in childhood?

Busy schedules and fast-food attitudes have greatly limited times for adult conversations with children. Television and electronic gadgets have also done great damage to conversation between adults and children. A few decades ago, families worked and talked together as a natural routine. Now we easily forget the crucial value of time to have such conversations. Studies suggest that adults in developed countries currently spend less than ten hours a week talking with children.

Whether our caregivers were authoritarian or authoritative further complicates how we learn to think as children. Authoritarian caregivers tend to teach children to follow their rules, not how to learn effective rules on their own. They basically demand behaviors that they think are helpful. For many, this leads to dangerous experiences and social failure once grown and out of the home. When we haven't learned to think through the consequences of our decisions, the expanse of options as a young adult is confounding.

Often we end up copying the failure our caregivers modeled. We don't usually learn to do things differently if the caregivers who claimed to be right about their decisions took over the control of our life. We are especially vulnerable to this issue in the preschool years, when we first learn to think.

Authoritative caregivers set the rules, but want children to understand them. Some are even willing to acknowledge that their rules aren't perfect. As mentioned before, authoritative parenting is mending, modeling, and mentoring. These caregivers provided guidance for learning, letting children explore solutions for living while keeping them safe. If they do a good job, children aren't as reliant on learning from trial and error, or from the ignorance of peers.

Tribal cultures, either prior to colonization or those still hidden from modernity, historically took time to raise their children, using an authoritative, not authoritarian, approach. Sociologists have been surprised by the secure attachment styles they've found in tribal communities unaffected by the modern world. The three genetic styles at birth may have been different for tribal people, but their community-style of parenting and authoritative training clearly ensured secure attachment styles of personality.

Because authoritarian parenting stunts children from learning to think for themselves, trial-and-error behaviors often don't improve. The most well-developed children still have some trial-and-error learning to do, and being able to think clearly about choices and consequences is a great advantage. Our sexual attitudes are a good example of this. If we learned at home that sex is about relationship, we would more likely find success in relationships that others fail to find. Many today seem to believe that sex is primarily for individual pleasure. This attitude, often seen in teenagers, adults, and modern expressions like movies, frequently leads to despair more often than happiness.

The work of life is best learned in a safe and supportive situation; that's how tribal people did the job for centuries. It's a poorly considered short-cut for parents to just insist children do things. Some of us learned many things the hard way after we left home, due to having had parents who took full responsibility for our behavior. If we don't learn to think for ourselves, and internalize some good rules, we may experience living that isn't easy, or very safe.

Also, when we learn behaviors from immature parents, we may quickly repeat their mistakes: Our marriages may crumble, employment may be troubling, and success can evade us. We may have seen the issues in our parents, but didn't realize what we learned, and what we haven't learned. Such lack of solid learning in childhood can leave us with only trial-and error learning. If we're lucky, we may realize we need to educate ourselves about the task of living well. Denial, using anything from blame to avoidance that our past is limiting our success, leads to feeling stuck, powerless, and despair.

EDUCATING OURSELVES

When behavior is demanded of us, we not only don't learn to think for ourselves, but also don't learn to be suspicious of the authoritarian views of others. If we're left with trial-and-error learning, we've lost our primary difference from other animals. Like the genes of animals, our genes are restructured by our experiences, but we're also capable of learning from intellectual history. Genetic restructuring without reviewing our history sets humans on a course of negative unconscious programming.

If we had authoritarian caregivers and teachers, we didn't learn to think about what works best, or even how to use that information. We might not continue in education, even if we graduate, and may instead learn from peers, some of whom are bullies. In fact, authoritarian caregivers can be named as bullies, and, if we don't have excellent resilience, the ostracism called bullying can be very destructive in our lives.

When we break the denial-effects of authoritarianism, we more easily notice that education for living is widely available. We can sometimes find it in friends, family, books, and even in Googled items. The education needs to be tested. Those of us who believe that history books are too often more propaganda than history have learned that education always requires critical thinking. Talking with others, and thinking for ourselves, requires us to check, even challenge, what we learn.

Denial of the damage from authoritarianism leads to practicing immature behaviors, and corrupts lives. When youth know or value little regarding social skills, they can easily end up spending seven-plus hours a day on electronic devices. That will prepare a few for certain occupations, like modern warfare, but most are wasting practice time that might make them exceptional in other fields of endeavor. And employment left for those who haven't trained themselves more broadly is likely to be boring.

These are just some of the issues we may have to accept and address if we're to find the hope and education needed to live a successful life. Some relief from helplessness may be offered by simply knowing that we can always learn things about the work of living. However, even trying to change doesn't help if we haven't learned how. I'll describe some thoughts about how we can successfully change, but first there's another critical issue to face.

THE ROLE OF OSTRACISM

We need to break the circle of authoritarianism leading to judgmentalism, to ostracism, and back to authoritarianism. Most of us face ostracism at several points in our lives. It can start before we even enter school. If our behaviors lead to toddlers not wanting to share toys with us we get told we don't belong. The problem can even be that we look different than them. We can learn not to be aggressive, but we can't do much about how we look.

We can feel ostracism from insecure people, naïve people, and institutions. Whether or not intentional, ostracism always hurts because it's in our face about our basic needs, especially belonging. Bullying is a form of ostracism that's easiest to spot, but it's only one form of many. All forms of ostracism not adequately resisted compound our feelings of ignorance.

Being ostracized can make our shortcomings and anxiety worse, which can debilitate learning. We may have found defenses for our weaknesses, but being ostracized can easily overpower them. We can then easily feel it's our fault that we don't belong, which damages all of our basic needs. Facing such rejection, we can move from belonging to alienation, from adequate self-esteem to worthlessness, from feeling in control to feeling helpless, and from life being meaningful to life being meaningless.

No one escapes ostracism, but people with difficult personalities, low levels of education, anything less than high levels of economic status, and those not appearing to be of a dominant culture suffer the most and the longest. In the extreme, they join violent gangs and drug-related groups to feel powerful and as if they belong. More commonly, long-term ostracism leads to deeming life as meaningless and not taking care of one's self, which may be a form of passive suicide.

Denial is especially risky when we experience ostracism. We must maintain strong defenses, and denial distracts us from such thoughts. Our resources for coping can be depleted when the experience is continual. Awareness can lead to getting support. The primary source for an adequate defense against rejection is having a supportive community, as well as knowing and accepting our personal history. When we have support of a community, knowing why we have shortcomings helps defend us against all forms of ostracism. Unfortunately, many have little or no community.

THE NEED FOR COMMUNITY

The ideas of family and community have been greatly damaged for many of us. The United States has emphasized, from its beginning, that individual effort is that which is rewarded. Here, governments, corporations, and sometimes families rarely take any responsibility for individuals. Families have been damaged by both poverty and affluence. Both conditions tend to keep us too busy to sustain a healthy family and community.

Can we overcome this burden to living successfully? In life, we have a lot of tough times, so we need to find the support of community, but even that can be difficult if our social skills are inadequate. Society is not kind to those with too many social limitations. For example, both shyness and arrogance easily diminish one's ability to experience community. We may have to begin by developing our own living skills before we're ready to gain community.

Thus we may have to start with individual responsibility. That's a bit ironic given the damage we can feel if we lack community. The first step might perhaps involve something as simple as remembering that a daily walk would be healthy, or to only turn on the television for planned and limited watching. The first task is to find something that will assist in our recovery from feeling helpless.

To act on our own behalf requires hope that we can act successfully. That seems impossible when we've tried and only experienced failure. How do we develop caring-behaviors for ourselves if we've had too few adequate models or other experiences for such actions? Like all behaviors that aren't just reflexes, love is an ability that has to be learned, especially self-love.

Self-esteem and a sense of belonging are both born and sustained in being loved. We can easily feel like we're dependent on the love of others, and that's true for children, but as soon as we become fully rational—by about fourteen years of age—we have the capability of rationally loving ourselves. Love isn't just emotion. Sometimes we think situations through and choose loving acts. The loving feeling normally follows loving acts, like being kind to someone.

Because we often think of love in a romantic context, it's easy to forget that love is an act, a behavior. Sometimes loving acts have nothing to do with feelings of love for another person. When we understand why someone's behaviors have left us not feeling any love for the person, we can still find it possible to act in a loving manner toward them.

We can easily miss these opportunities for loving acts because, after many failures, we might believe we cannot change. We might not understand how programmed we are, and might not have learned how important loving, including ourselves, is to feeling loved and being lovable. Having a supportive community might make trial attempts at loving acts easier, but these acts can be done by rationally thinking through the situation.

For example, when people aren't easy to love we need to understand the challenges they face. Not denying causes of relationship difficulties, we can usually find it in ourselves to visit and express other acts of love. As long as we're careful to mind our own needs as well, caring for those who are difficult to love can help us with meaning and worthwhileness, two of the primary elements of personal happiness.

To have loving behaviors for ourselves, we need to start by considering that our feelings that we aren't loved, or are otherwise not worthwhile, are a mistake. Noticing negative thoughts needs to lead to a brief accounting of the damage we have experienced from the authoritarian world. If we just accept this huge mistake in thinking poorly of ourselves, we deny all four crucial factors of happiness: being worthwhile, belonging, controlling ourselves, and having meaning in our lives. As mature thinkers, we can correct this all-too-common mistake; it's a matter of educating ourselves.

A STARTING PLACE

The best starting place may be to work on acceptance of any damage from the past. This effort helps us choose to avoid blaming ourselves. Such blaming is self-ostracism. We need to take time to consider how well we've actually done, given the events that we may have experienced in our lives. We don't need Holy Scriptures to tell us that all children are to be loved. It's also fairly easy to see that if children didn't receive adequate love, they are going to be dramatically affected as adults, and so will be their own parenting style.

It's not easy to understand that adults who experienced damage can change. We need to remember that patience and perseverance are necessary for adults to be successful, to experience some control over their lives. We need to accept that being aware of our history is crucial, but not easy, if we're to be happy. The first focus needs to be on learning how we got to this damaged place, so we can understand the power we now have to do something about our situation.

We may be amazed how easily we forget to remember, or find excuses not to remember, our background. That's how denial works. Our belief in the process will be sorely tested. Of most importance will be to catch when we blame ourselves. Old habits don't just fade away; they have to be challenged again and again, and this can take years.

How often have we sighed in despair, let alone called ourself stupid. How often said *we should have known that*. Then there's the *I can't do that,* and other statements doubting our ability before we even try or study the problem. Yes, it's scary to think we can do something new after a season of failure, and new activities need fair and honest consideration, but finding success overcomes this denial. And, progress leads to both happiness and more freedom from denial.

The fact that personal change can take years is one of the discouragements that can lead us to giving up. But to give up on this process is to give up control. It's important to understand that living is a process, and being an agent of the process can help us overcome feelings of helplessness. When we feel even a fledgling sense of having some control, we may be able to find healthy community.

Enough of us share the challenges of overcoming habits, that if we approach the subject without being judgmental, we may find a strong connection with others struggling to live successfully. That doesn't mean our community needs to be a therapy group, it means that community can be built around understanding and acceptance.

Lack of understanding and acceptance hinders many relationships at work and in social places. But imagine if we participated in society without ostracism—receiving it or perpetrating it. Ostracism, as we've seen it, is about insecurity; it's a defense. It restricts and limits relationships. Acknowledging a problem, and working to understand and find relief from it, can lead to winning friends. Found to be someone who has learned not to ostracize others would be quite appealing.

Because even one friend can be community, we may find it important to educate ourselves about the work of friendship. It will be helpful to anticipate that we will need to accept that training is necessary for the task, just as in other elements of life. The community discussed here is when at least two people put caring for the other as second in importance only to caring for themselves. If caring for ourselves is put second, the community is usually corrupted and will lack trust. This issue means that we'll need energy left after meeting our own needs or we won't have resources left for a friendship. Like most others, we may be busy, but making time for a friend helps us gain the all-important support of community.

Finding good models for friendship can be difficult. Recognizing a good friendship may be difficult for a person who has never experienced one. Often, even our caregivers didn't maintain good friendship with each other. Many relationships today appear to be anything but balanced. Being in love with someone, which can often be felt right away and for poorly understood reasons, isn't enough for a good relationship. For example, being with someone who doesn't seem to care if the give and take of the relationship is balanced isn't a healthy relationship, even if you think you're lovers.

Time and talk are essential for healthy relationships. Relationships keep getting better with time and talk, especially if listening, understanding, and caring are also present. We all need to understand that we're not perfect, and that we have to work at our relationships. Thus, if we're to take this life-supporting leap of faith, our first task is to get ourselves in control of our desperation and despair. Again, we do this by accepting that we're responsible, but not to blame, for the life we're in. Sometimes, being responsible for ourselves is all we have energy for. And when we're that strained, we can easily feel helpless as well, but we need to remind ourselves that we're not.

Small steps for fledgling successes can overturn our feelings of helplessness and start us on our journey toward community. Occasional happiness will then result from being an agent of our own change. Life has meaning when we know we can learn to live well. Just as in life, we would be in despair in a game of chess if we only knew how to move the pieces. We also need to learn that strategies help us win.

When we develop some confidence in ourselves, we're far more likely to find a community, even if it's just one other person. With new-found control, no matter how minimal, and community, no matter how small, we develop resilience. Life is difficult. Resilience is crucial, and it comes from believing in ourselves. As we've noted before, being impatient with ourselves is self-ostracism, and makes life far too hard.

We can only truly believe in ourselves when we've accepted our limitations and struggles. Anything else is avoidance or outright denial. Defending ourselves with anything other than the truth can work, but doesn't make us secure. Then we can become susceptible to blame and bullying. And, if we blame others, we easily use this technique on ourselves.

We aren't empathetic when we blame ourselves and others. Empathy is seen as the ability to understand a person's situation and behavior. Blame just affirms that we think we're entirely in control of what we're doing. That's not clear thinking because most of our behaviors are unconsciously driven and well-practiced. No matter what our intelligence, we are never stupid, just poorly educated about the work of living.

STEPS TOWARD HAPPINESS

When we find that we don't adequately like our life, and can't find a way to change our situation, is it possible to go from hopelessness to happiness? Yes! We must remember that happiness isn't a place; it isn't even a goal. Happiness is a result. It's actually easy to achieve, though fleeting at first. We need to act and be successful. We have been reviewing just a few of the many obstacles to this simple behavior. Accepting that our life has been hard is the first step. Then we need some understanding to choose the next steps.

All along this path of life-progress it will be crucial to understand the psychology of denial. Denial has many forms and many causes. We often have to develop personal strengths if we're to effectively and consistently overcome denial. Denial can completely make a problem invisible. It can easily lead us to think that some strategy is working when it isn't. And, it's easy to deny that we're denying, especially when we're attempting to block a fear of trying something new.

We especially need not to deny that, like taking on any task when learning is new, the next steps will be difficult, and may feel impossible. Avoiding blame toward ourselves and others is critical at this point, as this may be something that has held us in check for too long. Knowing why our life is hard can easily leave us feeling depressed until we realize that overcoming difficulty has the greatest of rewards: happiness. Once we experience even a little success, a fleeting happiness, we will find it a little easier to accept that we must work at living. Even knowing that we have things to learn can feel less helpless than just accepting our fate.

After acceptance, we need motivation or denial will likely reign again. We may need assistance with motivation, but we can do it alone. We won't find motivation unless we risk the idea that allowing despair is a mistake. If we've lived in despair a long time, we might find it challenging to admit that we had been that wrong about our life. We may have felt completely responsible for our lives, with many others encouraging us to think that way.

If we're going to be responsible people, we must understand *what* we're really responsible for in our lives. We're responsible for thinking problems through, and doing something about them. We're not responsible for how we learned to have the problems. If we find we've been numbing out with TV drugs, sex, or you name it, we need a gentle approach for taking responsibility for letting go of activities that, in the short term, have given us comfort.

It is exactly at this point that we may need not to be in denial of the damage we may have received from this authoritarian world. If our predominate experiences have been demand and punish combined, starting in childhood, with unrealistic expectations, then we're likely to be denying by self-blame and lowered self-expectations. Then we've step off the road to happiness.

Steps to happiness begin with just wondering if we've been missing something. Wondering if our life experiences could have been a mistake. Then we need to research the causes of failure and frustration. We often have some damage repair to do before we can sustain travel on the road to happiness. Getting others who are out of denial about their human frailty to join us on this journey can be quite helpful.

THE EFFECTS OF PERSONAL EDUCATION

1. Alienation becomes belonging.

2. Helplessness becomes control.

3. Worthlessness becomes self-esteem.

4. Meaninglessness becomes meaning.

STEPS THAT MAY DEEPEN UNDERSTANDING

1. Consider how much of our thinking is out of our control, and how despair is a problem of not knowing how to change our life.

2. Reflect on where we may have fallen back on unconscious patterns when trying to change.

3. Think through the importance of community.

4. Review the relevance of the prior chapters in this book.

5. Evaluate what a leap of faith would be for us.

The world as we have created it
is a process of our thinking.
It cannot be changed
without changing our thinking.

Albert Einstein

CHAPTER TEN
PERSPECTIVE

Readers may conclude many things as they read this book. We each have our individual perspectives on life, and how to live it. My hope is that a central conclusion for all of us is that denial can imprison our lives, and that we can take actions to limit such a sentence. Understanding and correcting negative issues of denial is a central aspect of making changes in our lives. Understanding denial helps us determine whether we see our lives as givens, or as works in process. With this awareness, we recognize the effectiveness of maturity as something we work at, not just something others have.

Perspective is the ability to see meaningful pieces of information in relationship to each other. It is the most difficult to achieve when we have numerous pieces of important information. Life is basically indescribable with any sense of totality. When we're secure enough, we enjoy the mystery. We often find several perspectives on life, and how to live, within ourselves. Recognizing the presence and effects of denial has been presented as a most important perspective for success at living.

Life can force limited perspectives on us, like when we're forced to focus on basic survival, but we must still regularly consider denial as an important element. It is seldom irrelevant to our living. Noticing denial is itself a basic survival skill. Believing that you just have to take life as it comes is denying the value of working at it, and the despair that comes with such a view limits the vitality of being human.

If our early childhood caregivers did everything for us, and perhaps continued into later years, we might not be able to grasp this denial focus until we learn a work ethic. If some event, or good friend, encourages us to try working at life, the first success will be the hardest. We just won't know the value of work. It will take a leap of faith out of our despair, or the trust of a friend willing to support our attempts without doing anything more for us.

Those of us with a good work ethic will find it much easier to mature once we clearly see the importance of this focus on denial. We'll find it easier to believe in ourselves. We'll already have had other successes in our lives. It'll be easier to expect that life can be more, happiness more encompassing, and that quality of life isn't a given, but gained by work. Success from our own work is a powerful motivator.

This denial perspective isn't about what we have accomplished, but that we've found we can accomplish. As we've seen in several chapters, happiness is about progress on the journey, not levels of aspiration. Accomplishment for itself can evaporate, leading to a feeling that life is fickle. We aren't always the makers of our fate, but we can strengthen our ability to affect change in our lives, and develop resilience for difficult times.

We're in the world where, when not in denial, many things are beyond our control, and being our agent for change when available supports at least our meaning, if not happiness itself. We may use this agency in a way that even brings our death, but we will have been really alive. We will have lived a life worth living. Such a perspective has more power if we believe in an afterlife, but I would present that even without such a belief a life well lived is of highest value.

When we see that we have agency, we need to think about what we are doing with our lives. Experiencing the ability to change opens our awareness of the meaning and purpose of our lives. Goal setting has been proven to help with obtainment, but it can be a limitation and disappointment when in denial. The goal of life needs to be the deep happiness of progress that radiates out of found meaning. When we limit our goals, our denial can lead to us holding them too inflexibly.

To see through a perspective of recognizing denial, we have to be all right as we are. We might relate our willingness to find impediments to our progress to the happiness we find in such success, not in a broader accomplishment. A perspective on accomplishment is too easily corrupted by ego, insecurities, and arrogance. Success is an individual matter, and comparison is usually misleading.

In fact, comparison is usually a symptom of our lack of understanding of how complex and often difficult life is. Colonizers and other war proponents used comparison to support their denial of their fellow humans who appeared different. It might appear we think of the homeless as less than us, or we might have done more for their situation by now. Comparison is often a form of self-righteousness in which we hide our denial of empathy and compassion.

This denial perspective is ground zero for the explosion of change. When habits lead to despair, we may feel there is no way out. Taking any small but successful step of positive change can be a life-changing experience, turning despair into progress and progress into happiness. Experiencing happiness can immensely change our lives. Yet, the medicine of happiness can fade. Our happiness needs to be constantly emergent. With denial restrained, we can be comfortable with the instability of happiness.

Emotions are very important to learning, though many educational systems seem to rarely notice. We need good feelings about ourselves, our abilities, and about the importance of a subject to optimize learning, or even to make it possible. When we don't develop such emotions in our childhood, we can develop them with this perspective on denial. Even small pieces of progress accumulate, and excitement for learning is contagious once it is found.

After we understand this role of denial, the steps for change become more natural with practice. We gently notice a negative habit reemerging. We use our empathy with this awareness so no negative labels are added to the problem. We then analyze where we erred and accept our mistakes. Having had prior successes, we won't fear this continued failure, but will develop a plan for noticing the context of the errors. Then we'll develop new rules, probably including rules about our failures. With each success we'll have more patience for change and feel our ability to change.

With denial restrained and happiness emergent, even boredom becomes one of the instigators of personal growth. Then quick fixes are more easily seen to be just frustrating responses to anxiety, and maintaining the status quo becomes a more obvious road to despair in a dynamic world. If readers have understood this book, they will understand why I believe that considering denial is a significant change to common ideas of how to approach stubborn negative habits. They will have found the life-journey of progress and find satisfaction.

This denial perspective can be challenged as making us take life too seriously. The live-and-let-live perspective tends to be the norm. Having a perspective for recognizing denial is based on the idea that true and lasting happiness comes from personal change. We usually don't notice that success can become boring. That's difficult to understand if you haven't had a high degree of success. Even small successes always peek and then diminish in importance over time.

The only infinite success is continual personal growth. It's a creation-tied perspective. Humans haven't been on the planet very long in this perspective, and have lots of room for growth. When growth provides happiness, there's no end to it. Eras of success diminish, but happiness continues to grow.

The time for using our denial perspective is any time that we feel we've failed at something, or that we're generally sad or just bored. Whether we're sad, bored, or even frightened about our lives, we need to ask *what am I in denial about.* Yes, the pressures and obstruction usually come from outside of ourselves, but the power to overcome them is always in us.

Some of us never learned a serious work-ethic. Some learned to work at projects, but not at living well. Overcoming denial is the work of living well. It's not about never being satisfied with our lives; it's about knowing we can have more. It's about learning that sadness and disappointment can't dominate our lives when we overcome the limitations of denial.

Fundamental progress has to do with the
reinterpretation of basic ideas.

Alfred North Whitehead

Epilogue

The Psychology of Denial is intended to generate discussion. I told a friend I hoped it would be a throw-away book if it generated enough discussion to gain significantly more clarity. I could have made this book a tome of thousands of pages, as I think almost every paragraph needs further discussion. Some clarity can be gained by more research on the many parts of denial that haven't been subjected to empirical query, but the topic will still need the input of many human lives as well.

There may be another book written in response to illustrations supplied by readers who see more than I've been able to understand at this point. Discovering denial in our lives is a journey, a life-long task that becomes enjoyable when happiness is obviously being enhanced.

"The universe is change;
our life is what
our thoughts make of it."

Marcus Aurelius

Appendix

DENIAL DESCRIPTORS

P. 3:   ". . . most of denial results from unconscious mental programs learned over a great period of time."

P. 5:   "Denial is such an abstract concept involving so many aspects of human behavior that it won't lend itself to even a broad generalization from research."

P.6:   ". . .we talk about denial in hindsight, yet we rarely recognize it at the time we are embroiled in it."

P. 6:   ". . . the stress of feeling stuck leads to denial."

P. 6:   "Denial is natural and necessary for human life, and most of it is unconscious."

P. 7:   "Denial is a good deal easier than standing against the crowd."

P. 7:   "Denial is a simple concept with many complexities."

P. 8:   "Clearly such indifference is denial, and a survival close to despair."

P. 12: "Denial inhibits our progress by shielding us from the truth."

P. 13: "Denial seems like a simple concept, and it's usually easy to see after the fact."

P. 15:   "Blame and exasperation are disguises of denial."

P. 17:   "Recognizing the role of denial in our lack of happiness is neither quick nor easy."

P. 19:   "Fear supports denial."

P. 21:   "Noticing denial is a first step in learning from mistakes."

P. 125: "In understanding that denial can be avoidance of intolerable thoughts, both conscious and unconscious, we can see that fear is primarily responsible for much of a person's denial"

P. 179: "Empathy allows us to inquire about our own lack of education, not lack of character, when we make a mistake."

P. 213: "Denial plays an important role in our repeated negative behaviors"

P. 219: "Denial often feels necessary when we're reduced to such feelings of despair."

P. 221: "Denial damages, even eliminates, our self-appraisal, our understanding of our part in things that go wrong."

P. 227: ". . .we're likely to take comfort in denial . . ."

P. 248: "Denial has many forms and many causes."

P. 253: ". . .denial can imprison our lives, . . ."

P. 253: "Understanding and correcting negative issues of denial is a central aspect of making changes in our lives."

P. 253: "Understanding denial helps us determine whether we see our lives as givens, or as works in process."

Made in the USA
Charleston, SC
20 March 2013